# NEEDLEWORK MONOGRAMS

## UNLIMITED: CONTEMPORARY STYLES

# B. BORSSUCK

**ARCO PUBLISHING, INC.**
**NEW YORK**

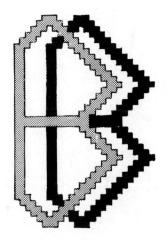

*All graphs and designs by the author.*

Published by Arco Publishing, Inc.
215 Park Avenue South, New York, N.Y. 10003

**Library of Congress Cataloging in Publication Data**

Borssuck, B.
  Needlework monograms unlimited.

  1. Embroidery—Patterns.  2. Monograms.  I. Title
TT773.B67        746.44        81-22937
ISBN 0-668-05453-0        AACR2

Printed in the United States of America

10  9  8  7  6  5  4  3  2  1

# CONTENTS

# INTRODUCTION

A monogram can establish visual communication in several ways. It can identify its wearer, declare ownership of an object, and, sometimes, imply authorship of a work. To perform these functions well, each letter should be clearly defined. Yet more sophisticated designs, unhampered by a need for legibility, can also convey messages. They can, like handwriting, reveal personality traits, expose artistic preferences, and proclaim individuality.

Roman lettering, never surpassed for simplicity, balanced proportions, and classic beauty, was used imaginatively in monograms. Letters were reversed, used upside down, or superimposed on each other. In the Victorian era, intertwined and intricately scrolled letters with the look of fine penmanship were in fashion and featured in the needlework manuals and magazines of the day, and monogramming reached a peak of popularity.

The alphabets here adapt characteristics of both of those periods and of typefaces used in today's graphic arts. There are refined styles that fit into geometric shapes—circles, triangles, diamonds, parallelograms—letters that interlace or intermesh, and bold styles for dramatic statements of identity. They are all expressly designed for use in arrangements, specifically monogram arrangements, rather than for use in word formations.

The modular or structural systems developed for the thirteen styles of alphabet presented in this collection will make it easy for even a novice designer to group any combination of two or three letters into unusual and attractive monograms in charted form, ready to use for any thread-counting type of needlework.

When designing with letters, great consideration should normally be given to the negative or background spaces in the composition. Or, to express the same problem in another way, letter spacing is very important, requiring a discerning eye and a skill that can be acquired only through practice.

Letter-arranging skill is not required when working with the units of the modular systems presented here. Instead of having to space a trio of letters of different shapes, you can arrange similar geometric units into patterns. In any pattern you devise, each unit can be replaced by any letter of the alphabet for that unit, even with *O'* and *Mc* in most styles.

Several sizes and compatible shapes of letters are included for each module. This multiplies the number of ways in which the letter can be arranged. The placement of a larger letter between two smaller letters will never be the problem you have encountered when working with standard letter manuals which give but one size for each style. The large choice of sizes will also increase your ability to fulfill special size and area requirements.

No longer inhibited and frustrated by a meager sampling of styles and sizes, or forced to accept two-letter instead of three-letter monograms, you can experiment freely. You can discover your creative abilities, gratify your desire for original styling, and produce spontaneous—or accidental—variations of classic modes and unique arrangements of unusual letter combinations. Your designs will be limited only by the scope of your imagination because the modular systems presented here are the working tools that make designing monograms easy and enjoyable. Hence, the use of the word *unlimited* in the title is justifiable.

There are no rules to follow when you design monograms. Again, your creativity is unlimited. Custom, however, does decree that the initial of the surname be the dominant letter of a group if there are inequalities of size, weight, or color.

All the alphabets are charted for thread-counting types of needlework on all kinds of canvas and evenweave fabrics. All graphs are on 5 x 5 squares to the centimeter (approximately 12 squares to the inch) graph paper. Letter sizes range from 12 to 72 squares high.

Each square space on a graph represents a canvas mesh or the crossing of a horizontal thread and a vertical thread. **Count spaces of a graph; count threads of the canvas or fabric.** In the charts, outlines of shaded areas and heavy lines that duplicate the lines of the graph paper do *not* represent stitches of any kind. They are used to accent the limits of areas and make the graphs easier to read and use. The arrowheads along the edges of a graph mark the centerlines of the letters.

When needleworked, the design you create will vary in size according to the mesh count (the number of threads in one inch) of the canvas or fabric you use. By counting the squares of your graphed design, you can calculate the size of the stitchery by applying this formula:

$$\frac{\textbf{Number of Stitches}}{\textbf{Mesh Count}} = \textbf{Size in Inches}$$

For example:

$$\frac{48 \text{ (number of stitches in height of letter)}}{12 \text{ (number of threads in one inch)}} = 4'' \text{ (height of letter)}$$

While designing with letters in graphed or charted form, needleworkers are apt to work much harder than is necessary. They will usually invest a great deal of time and detailed graphing on the first draft of a design, hopeful that it will be the last one. When (as is usually the case) improvements are possible or required, the novice will resort to using an eraser and destroy a good portion of the meticulous work done.

The experienced draftsman will cut and paste instead of erase. It is very easy to match and patch the printed lines of graph paper. Use mending tape—the invisible kind on which you can write—so that you can draw over the patched areas.

The advantages of the cut-and-paste method are twofold. It eliminates the need to redraw what has been done, and it makes it possible to experiment painlessly: to see and judge various spacings instantly, to try out different groupings, and to find new and more original solutions to the problems that made it necessary to rework the design.

You can use the match-and-patch method when you work with graph drawing paper (opaque), available in most stores that sell school and office supplies, or with graph tracing paper (transparent), available in art and drafting supply stores. Paper marked with green, orange, or black lines is preferable if you expect to make copies of your designs. Pale blue lines may not reproduce well on many copiers. Plain tracing paper will be very useful for making preliminary sketches directly from the charts, especially when developing ideas that

incorporate the overlapping, intertwining, or dovetailing of letters.

To take full advantage of the modular systems for which the alphabets are designed, use the cut-and-paste, match-and-patch methods or use any other procedure that will let you arrange and rearrange the units of a monogram quickly and easily without having to redraw them. You can also save much time and effort if you draw and work with the outline of the area or module common to a whole alphabet instead of with outlines of individual letters. Indicate the shape of the letter within the modular unit only if its unbalanced contour might stimulate original ideas of composition. Use a separate piece of paper for each element you might use in your design. Shift the bits of paper about, trying out every possible arrangement you can devise or stumble upon by accident. Line them up, stagger them, nest, overlap, superimpose or dovetail them. Fill in the details only when you are completely satisfied with your design.

If the design that has your final approval incorporates overlapped or intertwined letters, there are a number of ways to create the effect of several planes, one over the other, in your stitchery.

Different areas or planes can be made obvious by contrast. Contrasting colors or even different shades of the same color will produce the needed effect. The drawing of interlocked frames on page *132* illustrates the use of shades of the same color which, in this case, is gray. The play of light on different textures or stitch directions will also produce contrast and define the limits of adjoining areas, but with more subtlety.

A thin line of demarcation can separate two areas so that they may be interpreted as one over the other. Embroider a line over the completed needlework. It can be done in back stitch, split stitch, outline stitch, or any other that is suited to the work already done. The ground color may be used, but a lighter or darker tone of the color used for the letter itself will often be the better choice. Experiment to find the best treatment for the project being worked on.

Other ways that are especially useful for interpreting over-under sequences are the gate method and the shadow method.

Gates, used when letters are cut into stencils, ensure that the entire design and background are in one piece. For example, gates are used to connect the center oval in the letter *O* to the background, separating the letter into two arcs in the process. In the letter designs in this book, a gate is a space at least one stitch wide between two areas.

When the stitches of a gate are executed in a darker tone of the color used for the receding area, it is a shadow which helps define the over-under appearance of two planes. In the case of great contrast between the colors used for the design and the color used for the background, consider using the shadow treatment rather than the gate treatment.

The unlimited number of monograms you can design with the help of the graphs, ideas, and suggestions in this book can be used on silks, satins, velvets, and other close weaves as well as on canvas and evenweave fabrics. Waste canvas can be basted over the fabric to be embroidered to establish the grid needed for working a charted design; it can be removed, one thread at a time, from under the finished needlework. Waste canvas comes in a variety of thread counts; it is sometimes called breakaway canvas, which indicates the quality of this type of canvas.

Designs that have been planned and developed on graph paper can easily be transformed into line drawings for other kinds of embroidery than counted thread. Simply make a tracing of the design, smoothing out the steps and eliminating the jogs, so that the result is a free-flowing outline drawing which retains the basic shape and proportions of the graph. Reduce or enlarge it by mechanical means or by free-hand sketching to the needed size. Consult embroidery how-to books for methods of transferring designs to fabric. Once the fabric is marked, you can hand-or machine-embroider it in any stitch, style, or technique you deem suitable.

All the monograms shown in this book use letters exactly as they appear in the alphabet charts. You can do your designing without being limited in the same way. You may use letters as they are given, alter them, or bend them to your purpose. You can take advantage of unusual combinations and special cases to be creative and self-expressive. Let the monograms you design convey individuality.

A.E.B.

S.H.G.

K.M.F.

C.B.D.

L.O.N.

H.B.

C.E.V.

S.R.W.

Y.W.T.

W.N.P.

D.G.S.

H.B.H.

J.H.G.

A.McR.

E.R.G.

L.McD.

Y.S.C.

P.J.

A.C.E.

G.A.H.

S.G.E.

D.R.G.

F.H.K.

2

K.H.T.

E.G.G.

D.W.O.

C.G.

R.H.E.

S.C.D.

K.S.

G.R.M.

T.W.

N.F.N.

B.B.

B.B.

C.J.

F.E.B.

G.R.S.

P.H.M.

K.H.A.

3

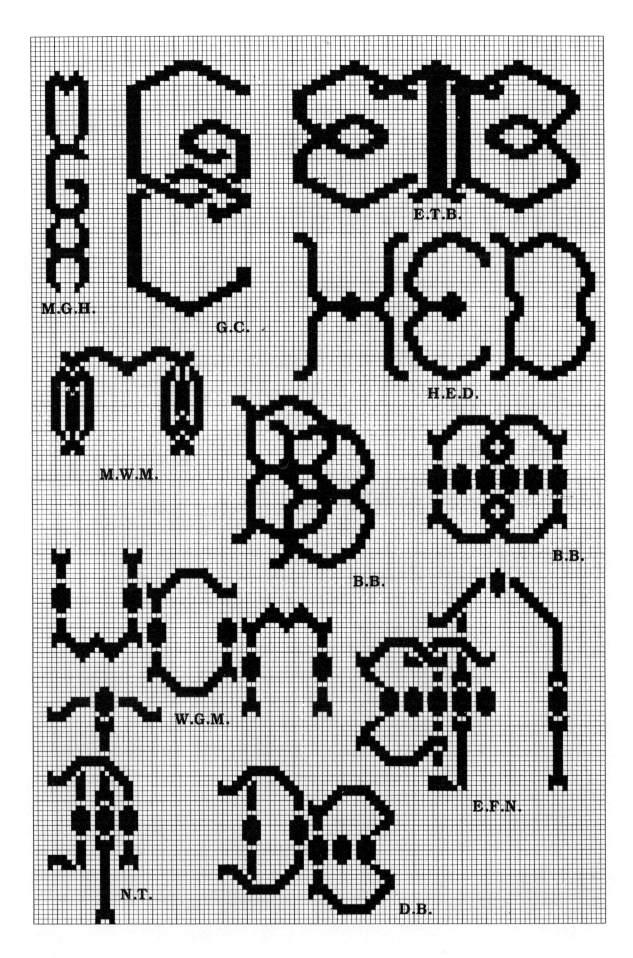

M.G.H.

G.C.

E.T.B.

H.E.D.

M.W.M.

B.B.

B.B.

W.G.M.

E.F.N.

N.T.

D.B.

4

**A.B.C.**

A monogram arranged within a circle is one of the most popular styles you can select. Perhaps its popularity stems from the fact that it satisfies one's search for perfect balance and symmetry.

In graphs, only an approximation of a perfect circle is possible. The smallest circle that would graph well and still accommodate any three letters of the alphabet was selected for this module. Your own monogram, no matter what letters must be used, will maintain the illusion of a circle and maintain good internal proportions when they are substituted for the *A.B.C.* of the sample.

Although letter size will depend upon the mesh or thread count of the canvas or fabric used, the area of the design in which these alphabets can be arranged will vary greatly, for it is possible to rearrange the three segments into which the circle is divided. The results can be unusual, but the curved contour of each letter will make almost any composition in which it is used pleasing to the eye. Letters like *F*, *I*, *J*, *L*, *P*, and *T*, with large gaps in their contours, will invite you to try off-balance treatments. The *FJ* monogram on the first page of the SAMPLES AND SUGGESTIONS section illustrates such usage.

Graphs of the letters *M* and *O* were eliminated because they may be easily adapted from the *Mc* and *O'* designs.

6

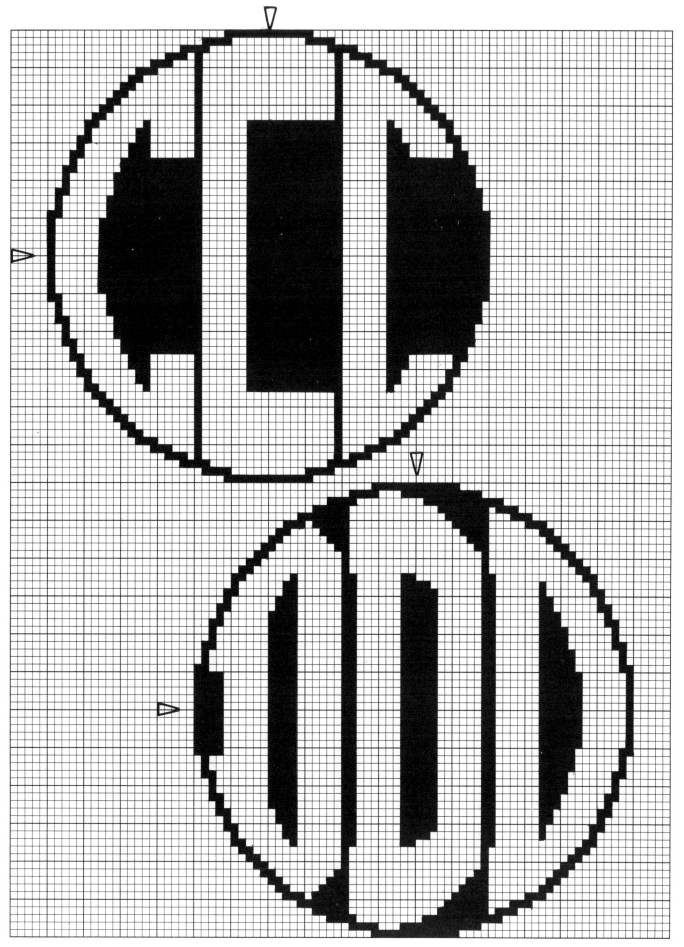

7

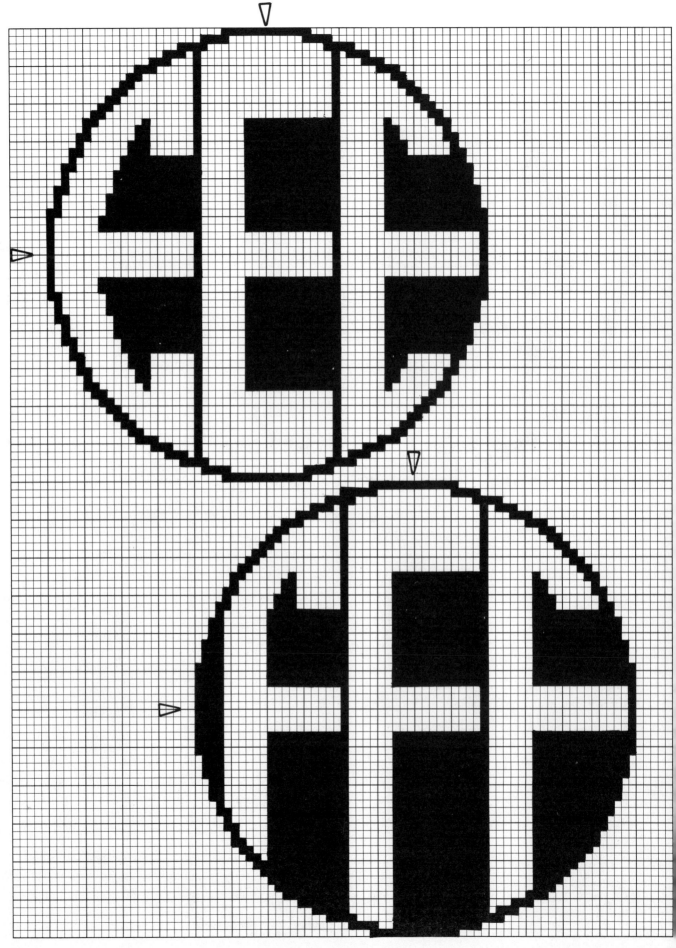

8

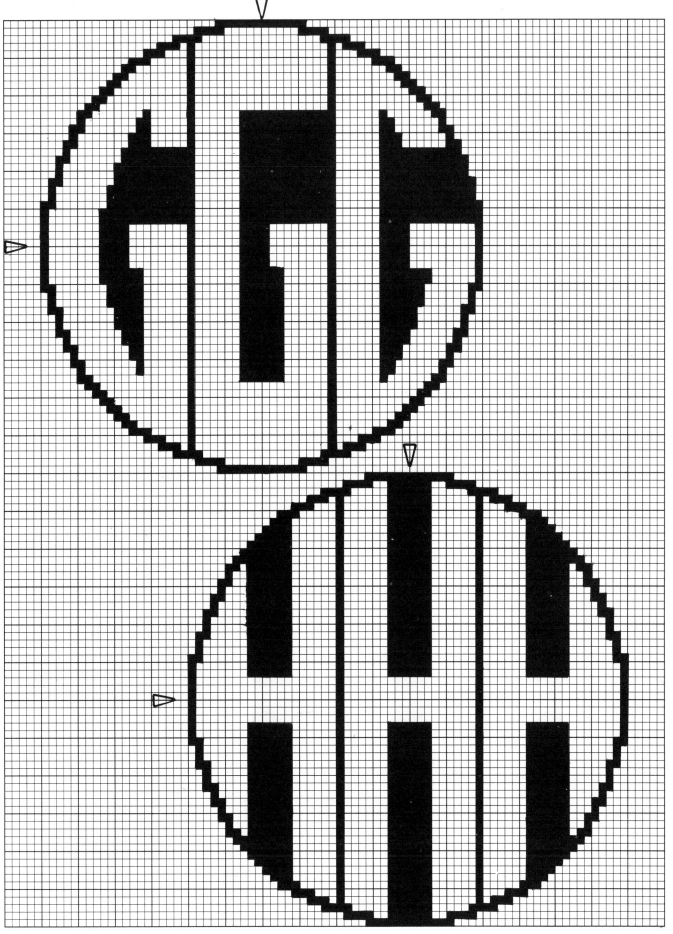

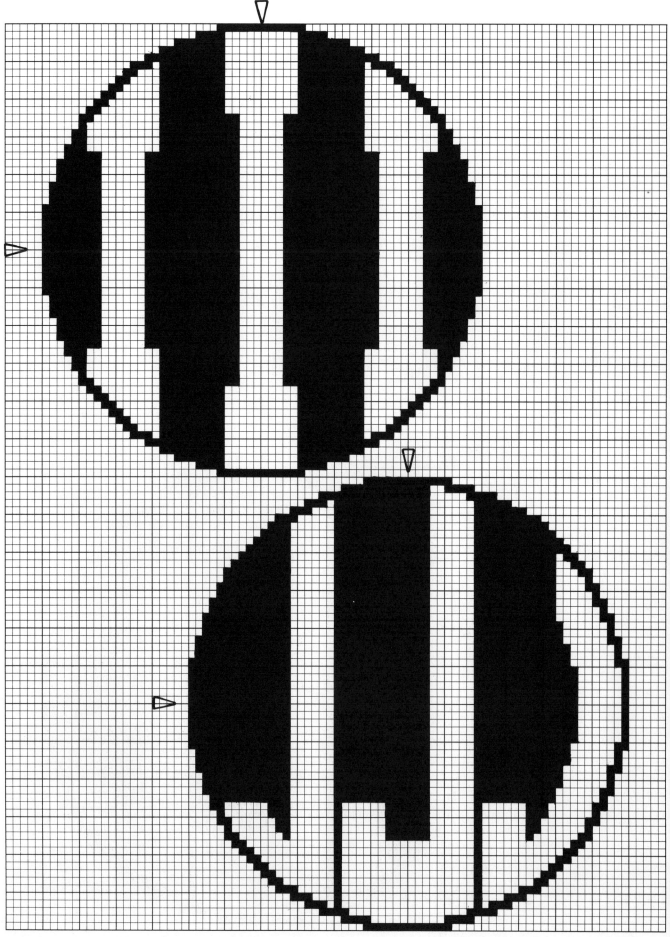

10

11

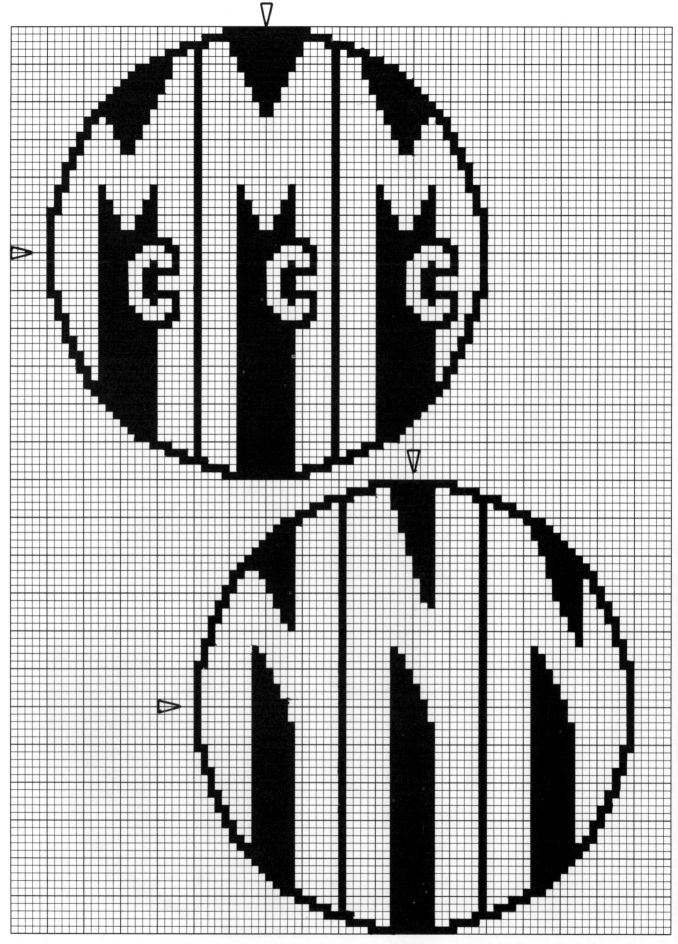

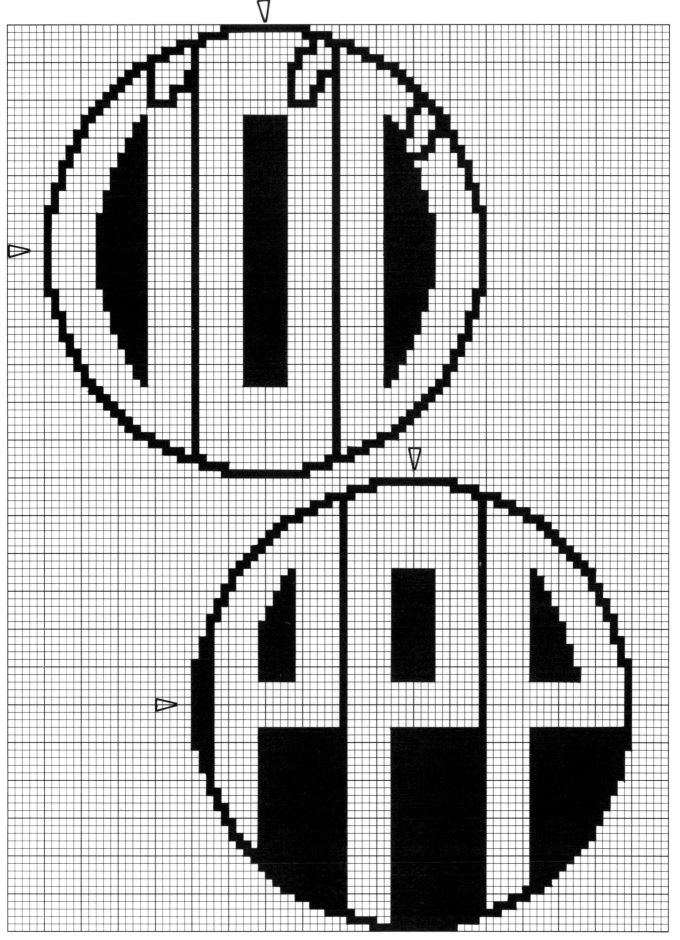

13

14

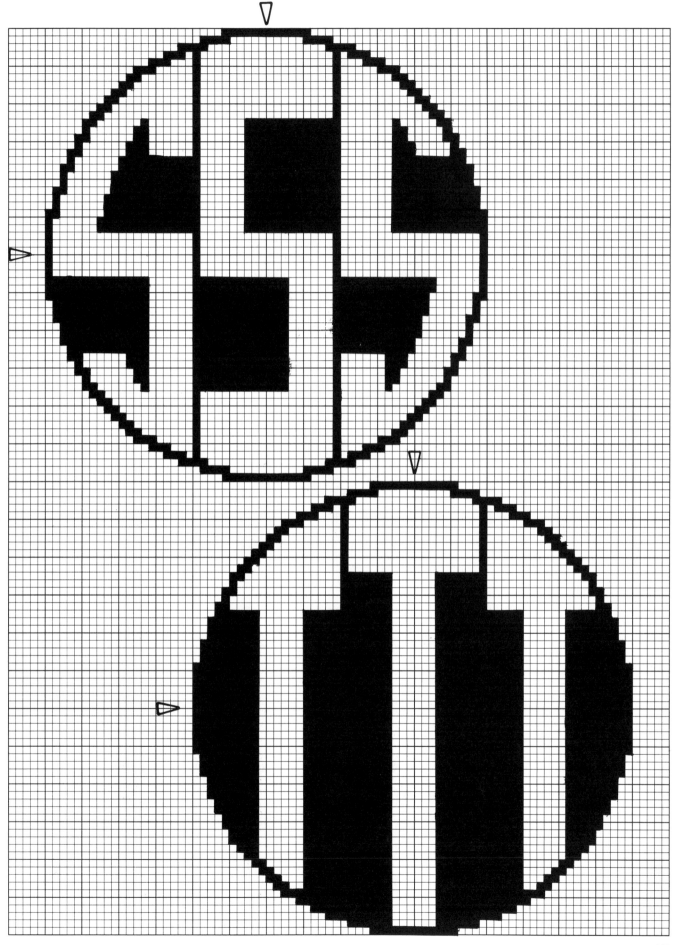

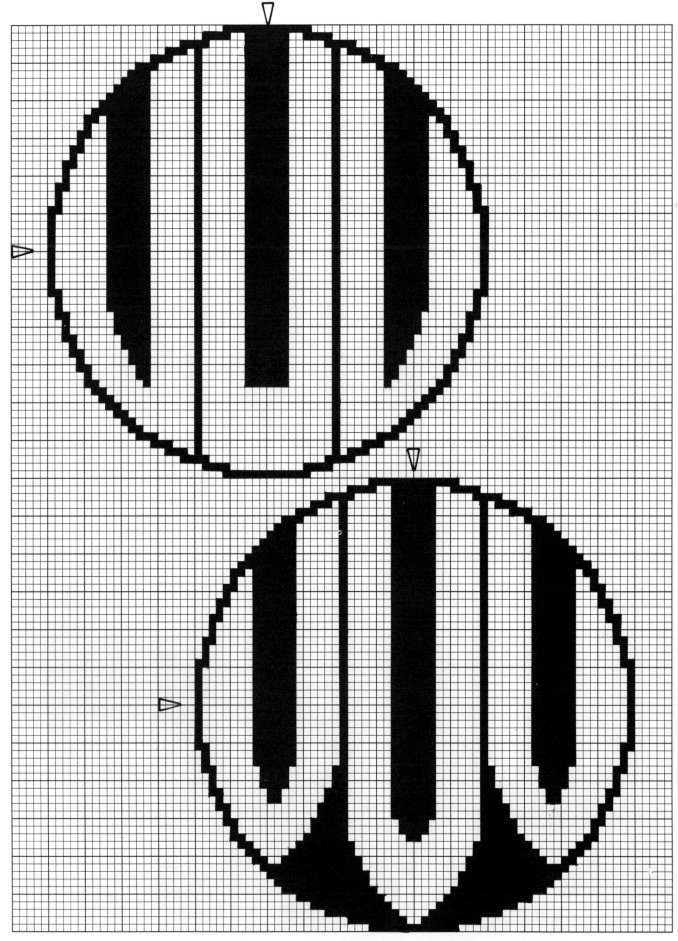

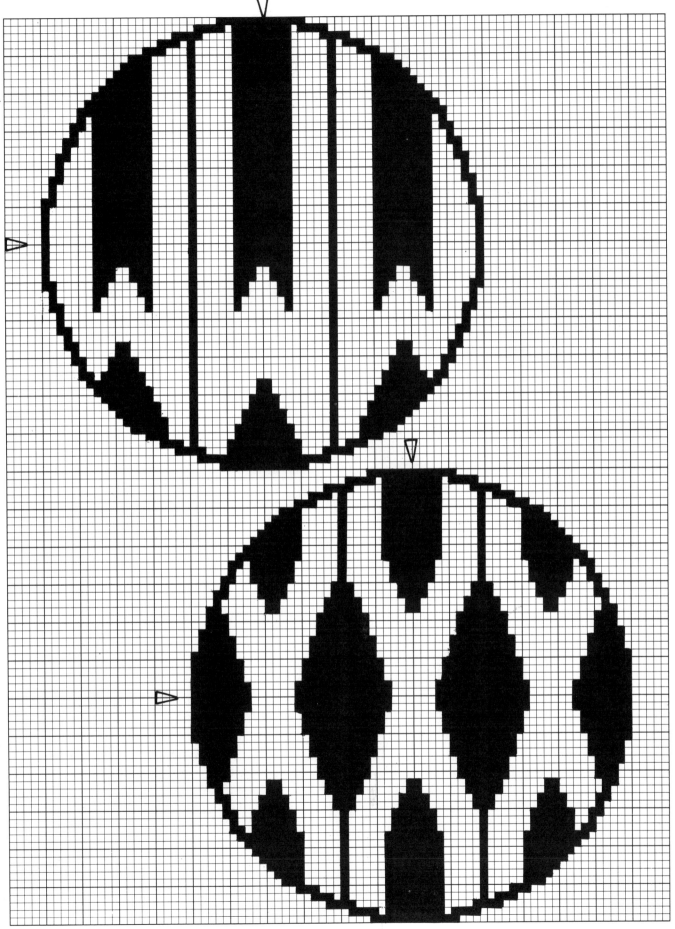

18

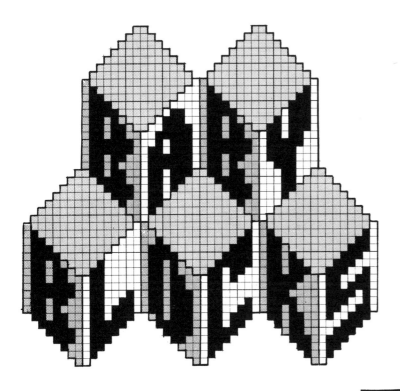

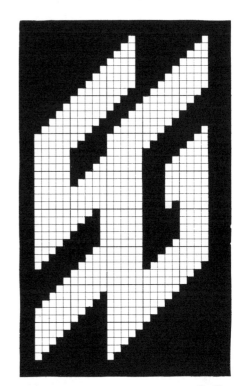

**S.G.**

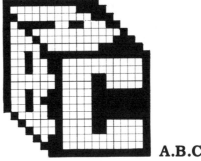

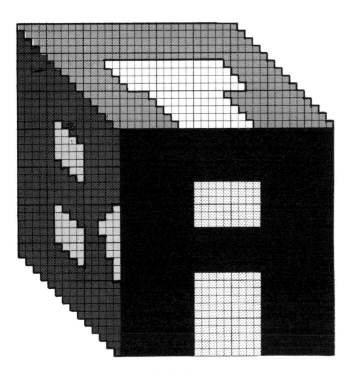

**C.B.A.**

**A.B.C.**

The large letters here may be substituted in most of the designs developed for the small size and give added opportunities for stitch variety and textural effects. The pattern for the large *O* was omitted in this module, but it may easily be derived from the *O'* charts.

Right-hand and left-hand slanting letters may be mixed or matched with the square letters. The ABC cube and the baby block pyramid illustrate such usages, and there are more suggestions for horizontal, vertical, and diagonal arrangements in the sample pages.

The letters in this module are compatible with many of those in the SQUARES AND RECTAN-GLES module, making it possible to design with letters of intermediate sizes.

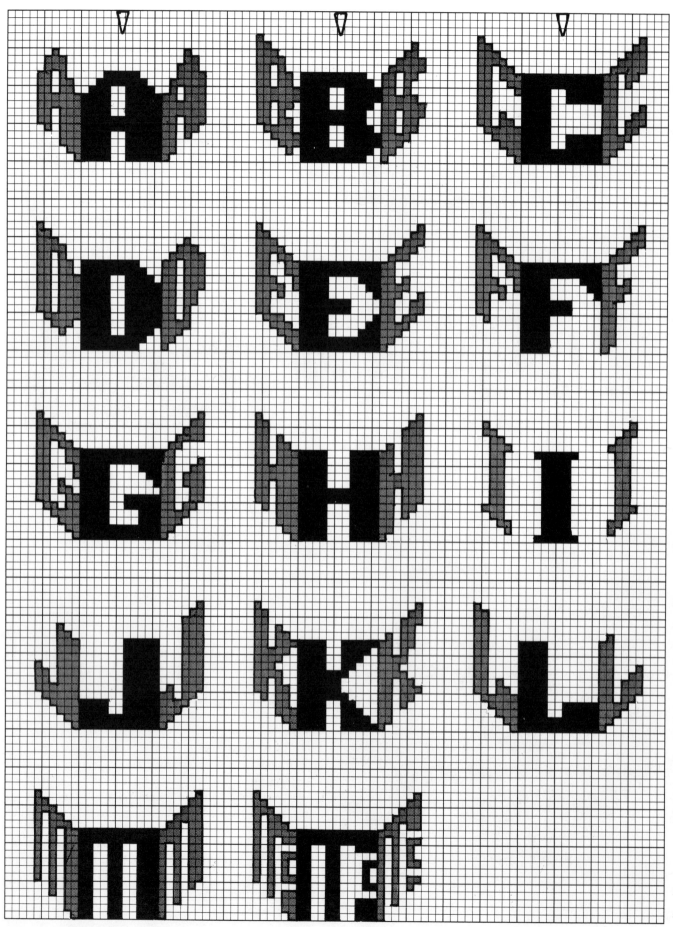

20

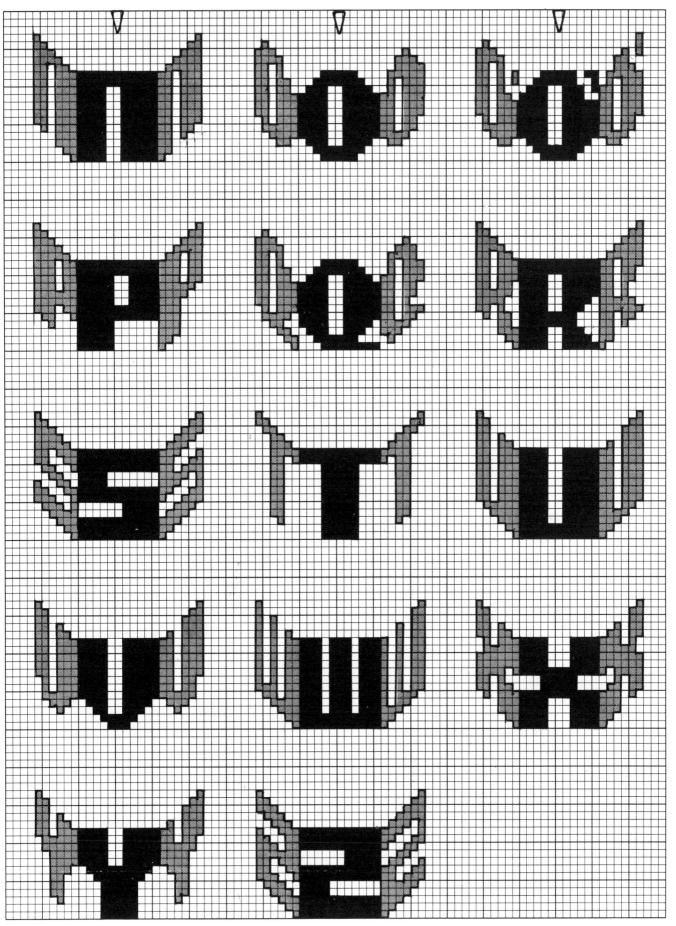

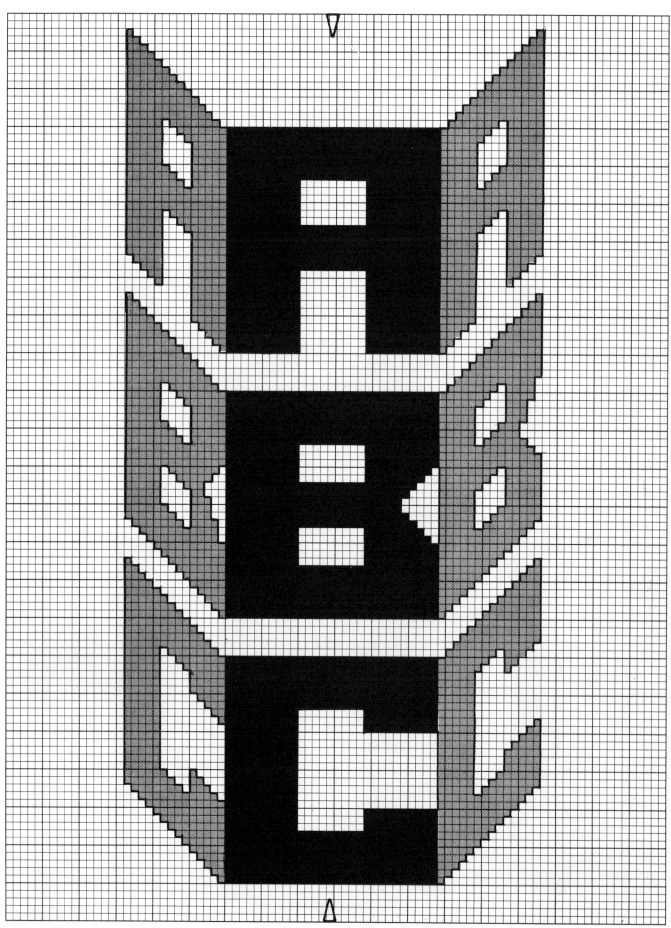

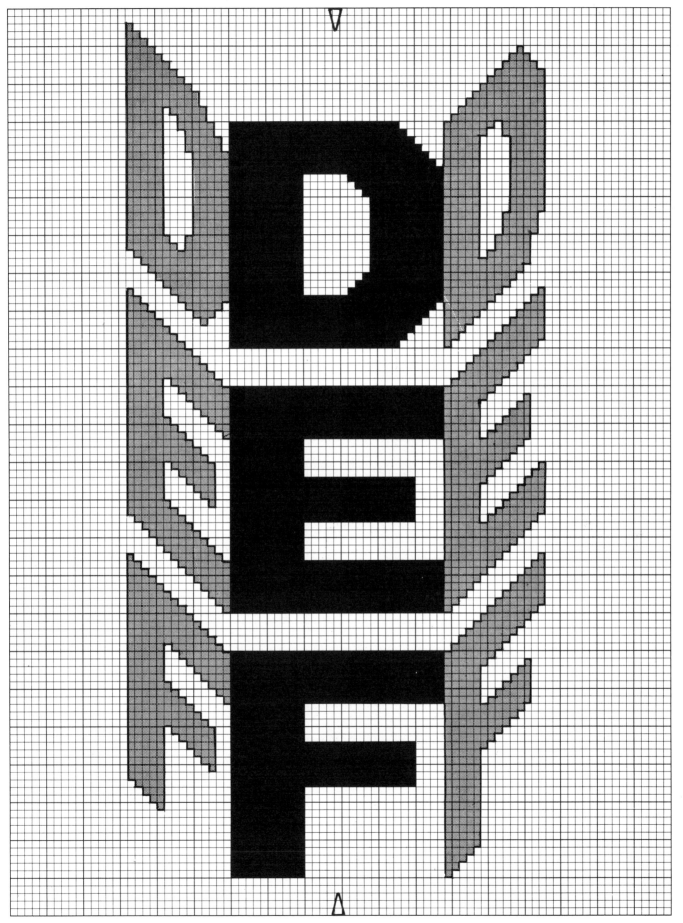

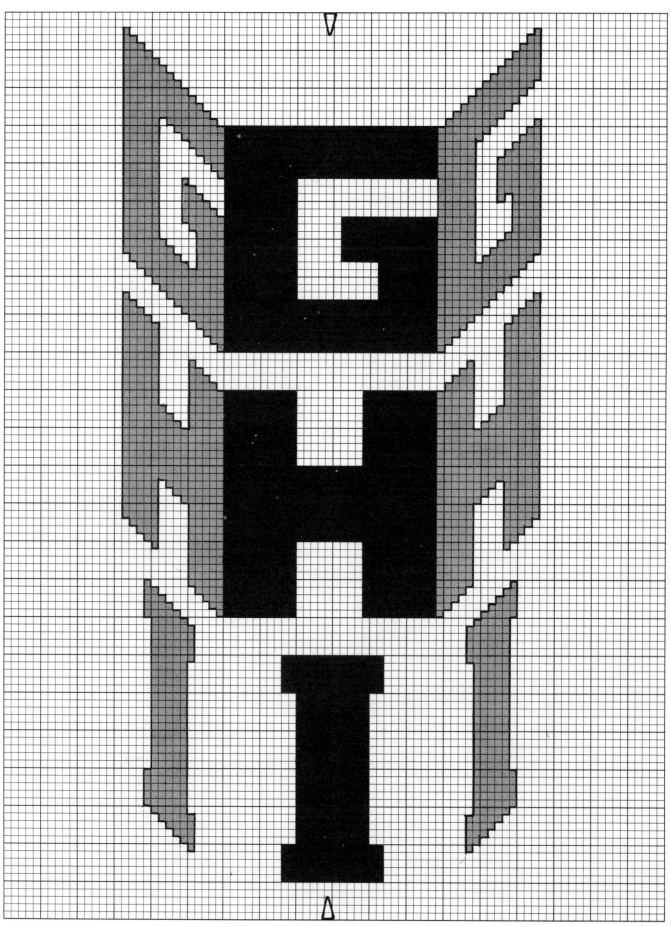

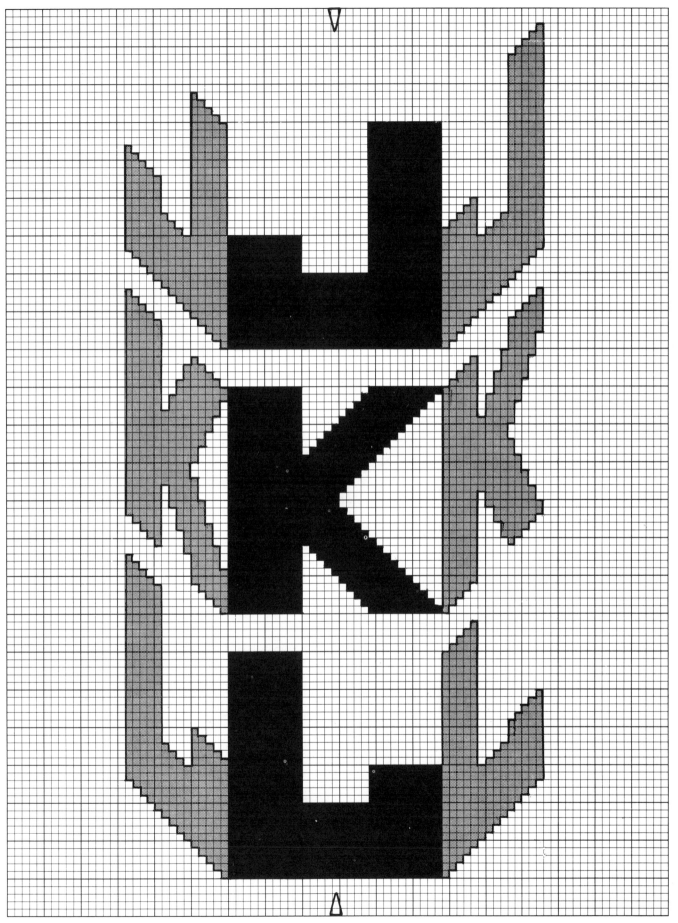

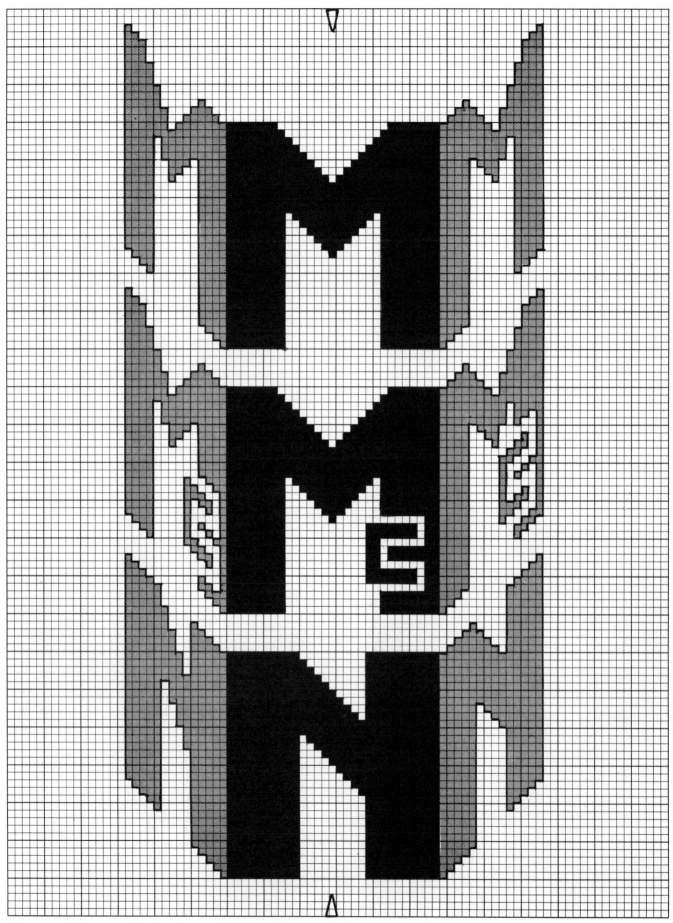

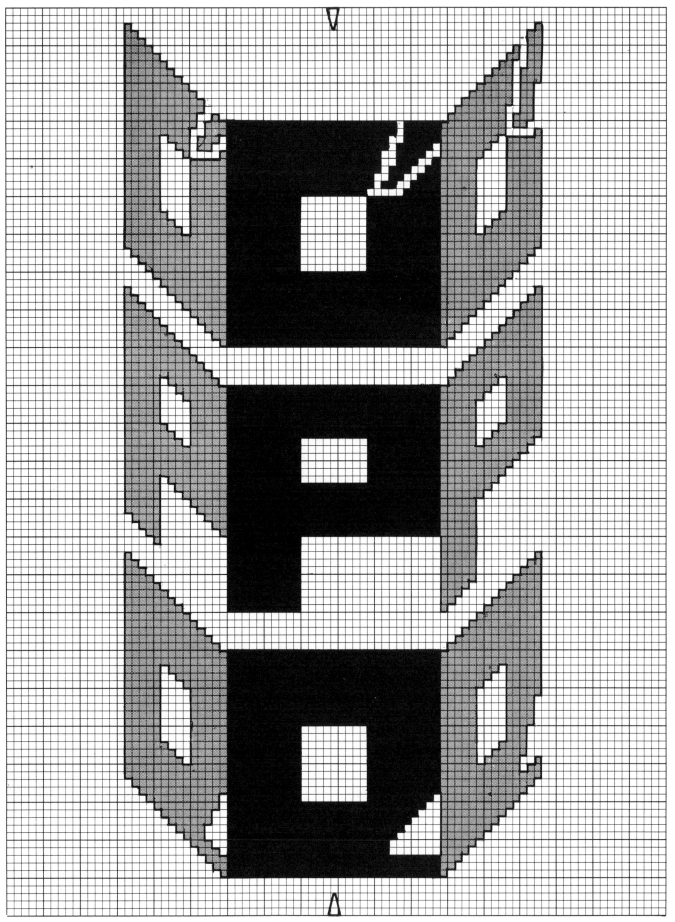

27

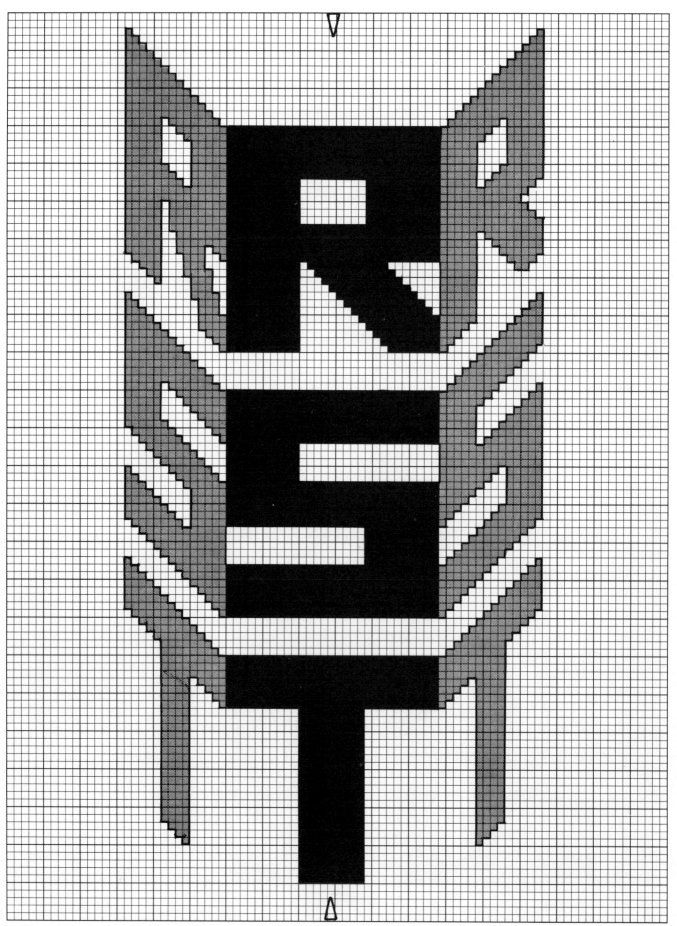

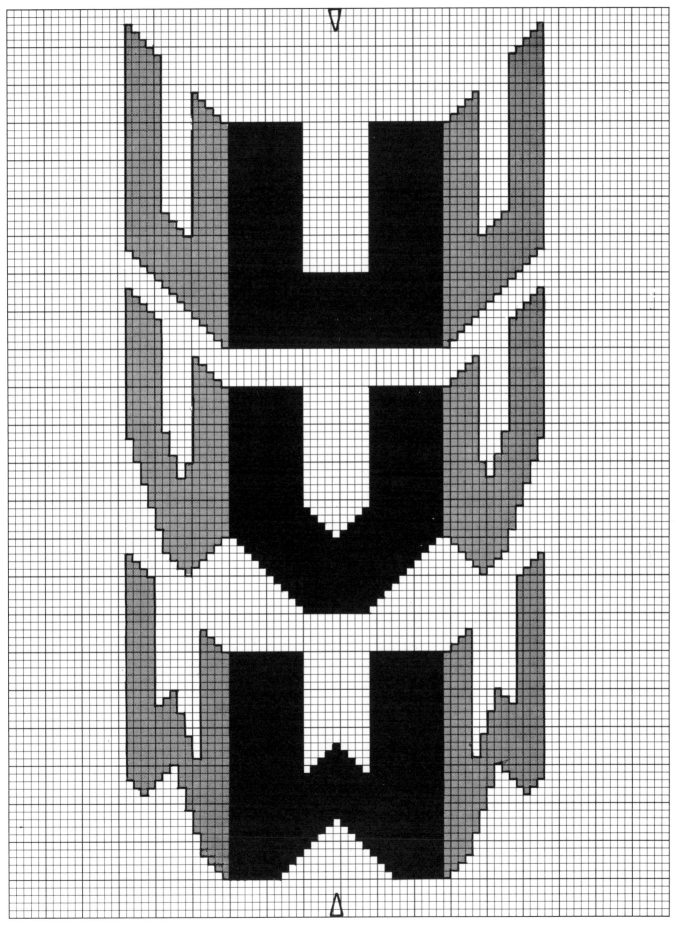

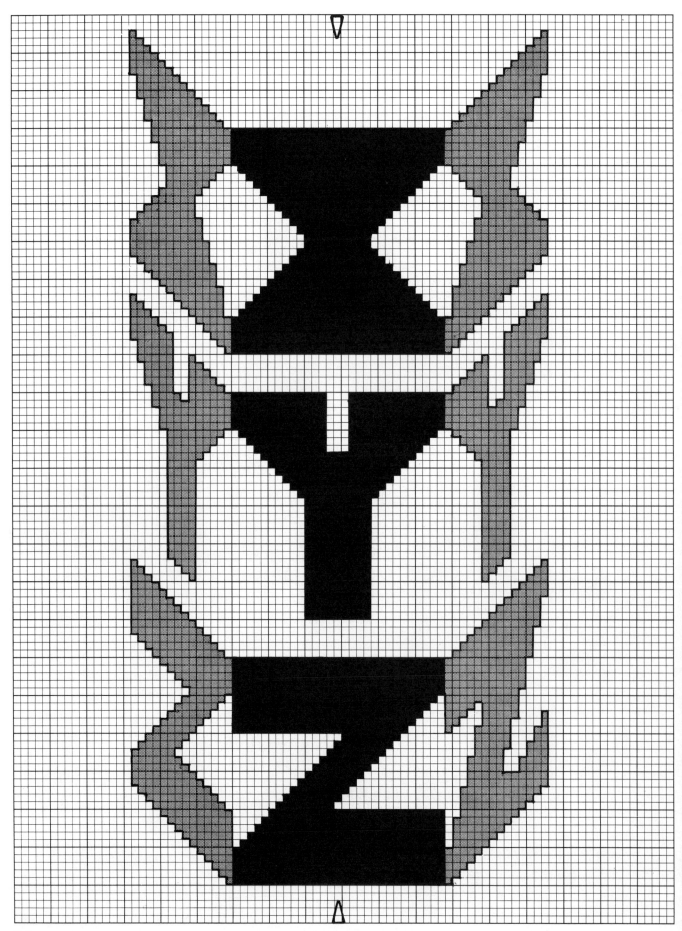

# Module 3  SQUARES AND RECTANGLES

M.N.K.

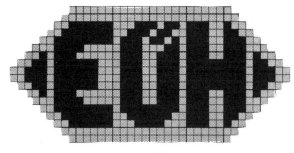

E.O'H.

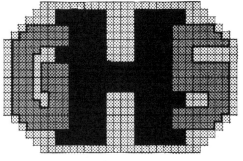

G.S.H.

Contemporary decor often needs simple, bold, block-like letters such as the 14 alphabets presented in this module. They are of different heights and thicknesses, but are compatible for mix-and-match selection. You can design for a very wide range of size requirements, since the letters are from 14 to 48 mesh high.

On the graphs, the diamonds at the ends of each line help determine the center of the letters in the line. The mitered corners of the end letters blend into the diamonds, but even when the diamond motif is eliminated, they help give a specifically-for-monogram look to the letters. The miters may be eliminated or enlarged to suit your design, and the center letters may also be mitered if desired.

There is no M page for this module, but by ignoring the small C on the Mc motifs, the shapes of each M will be obvious.

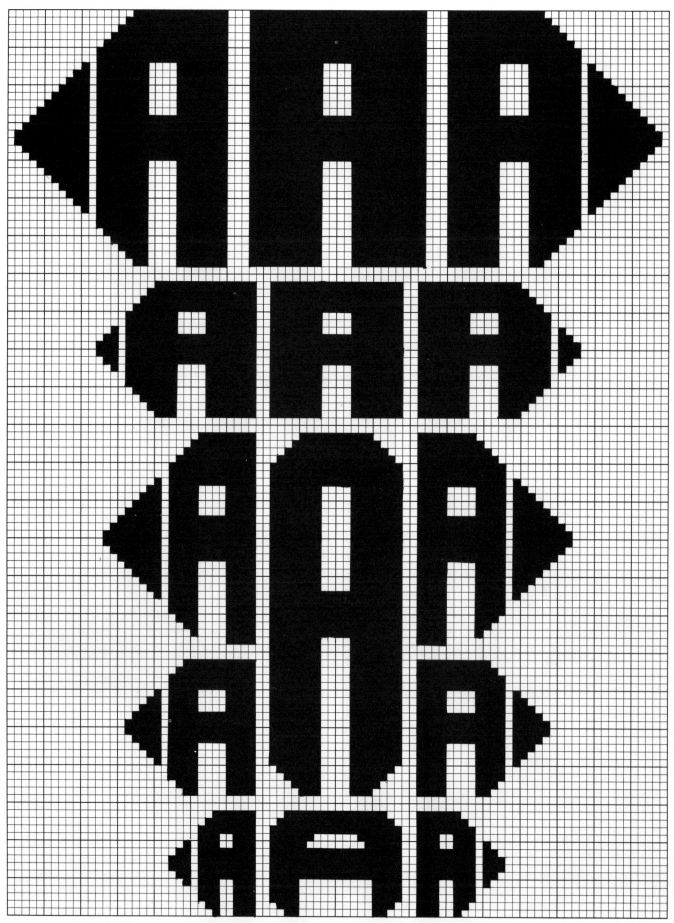

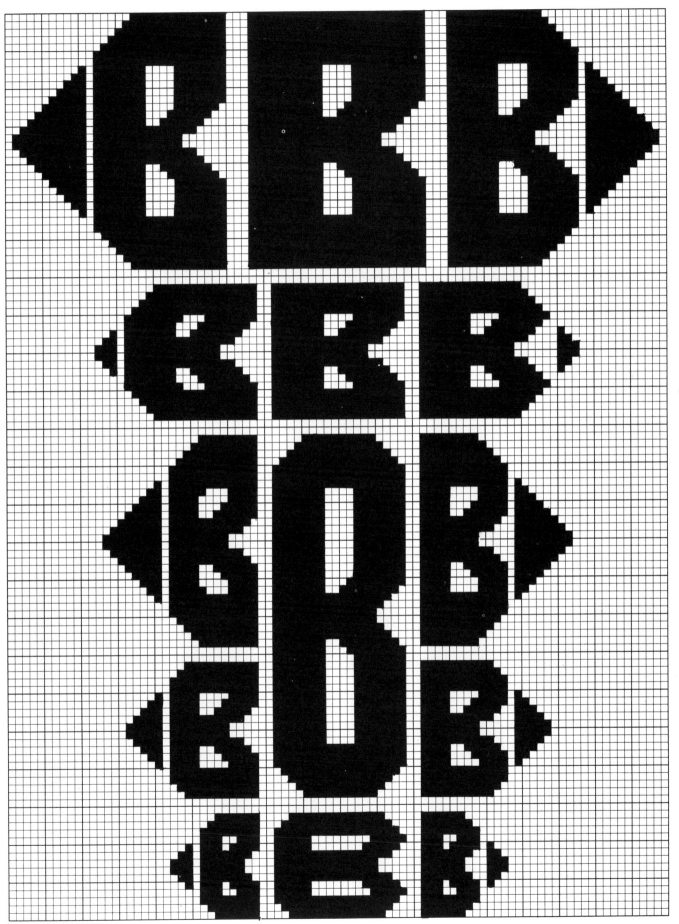

33

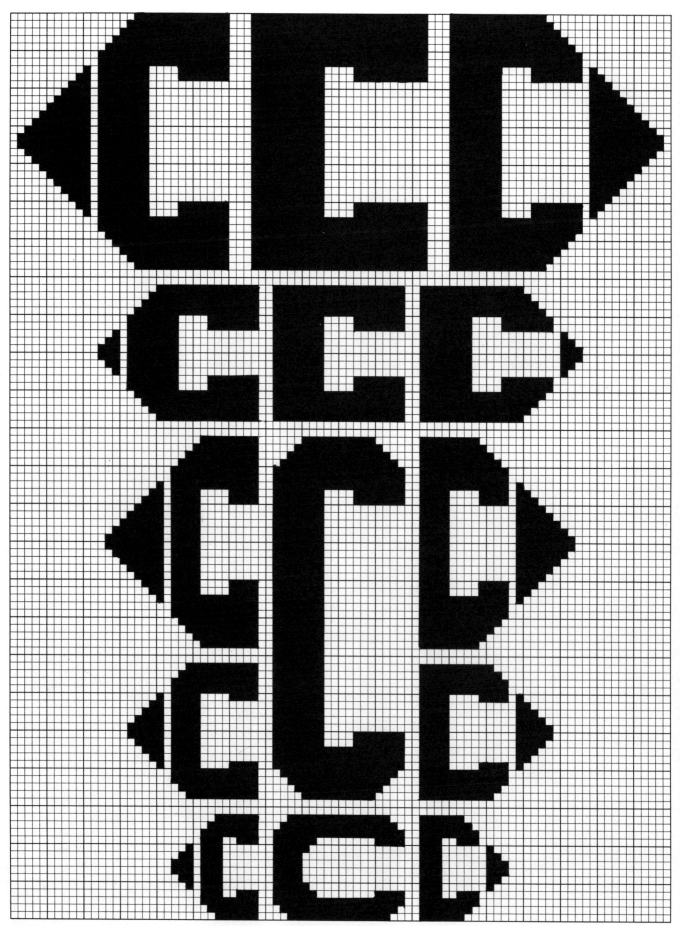

34

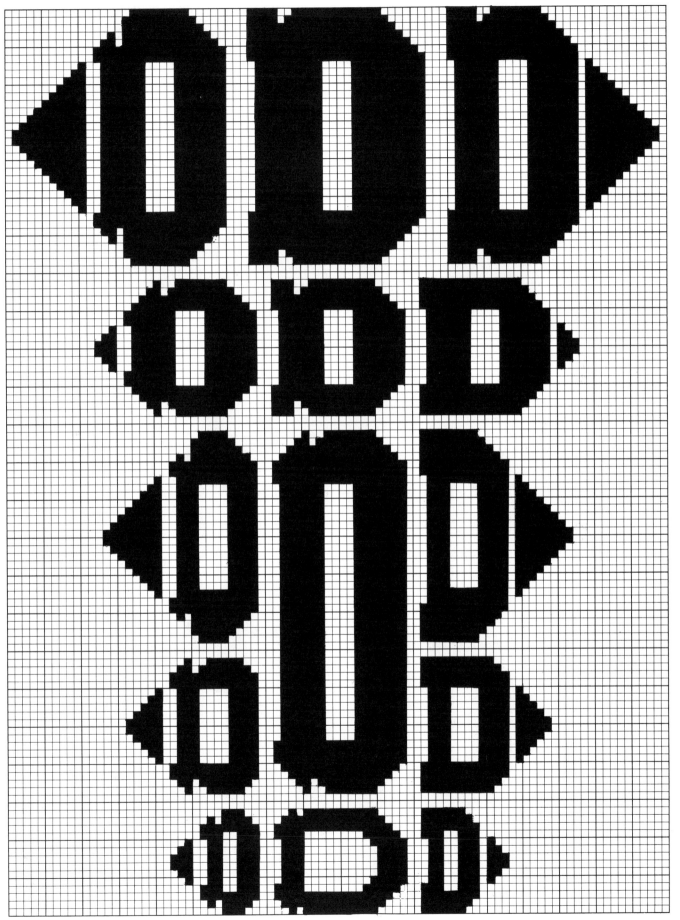

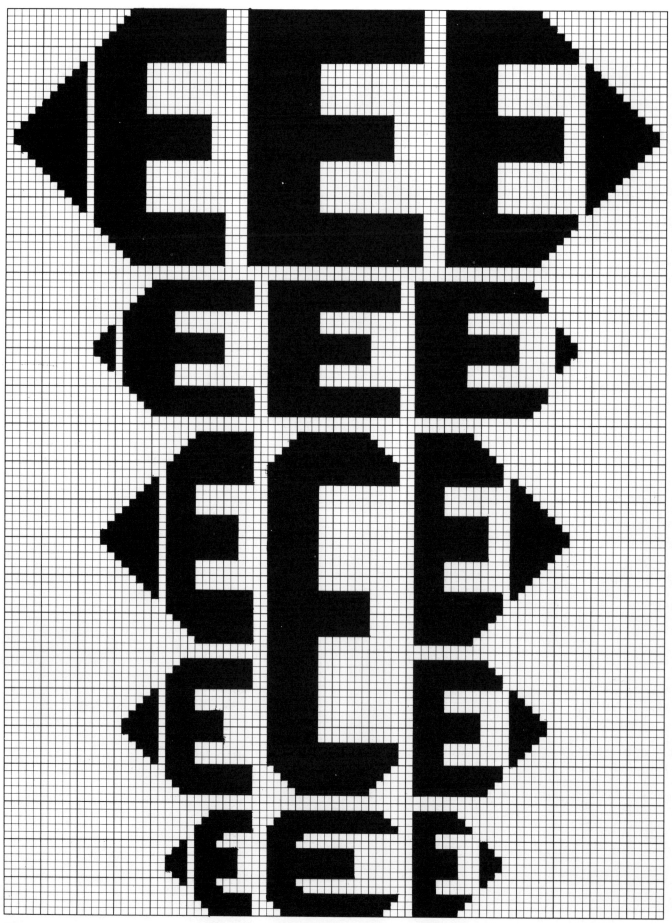

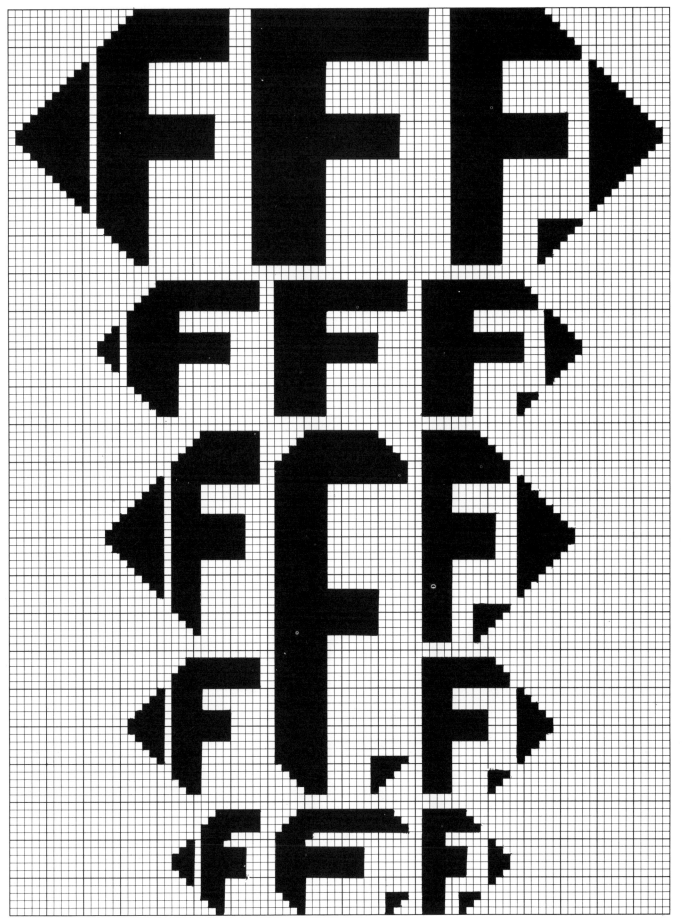

37

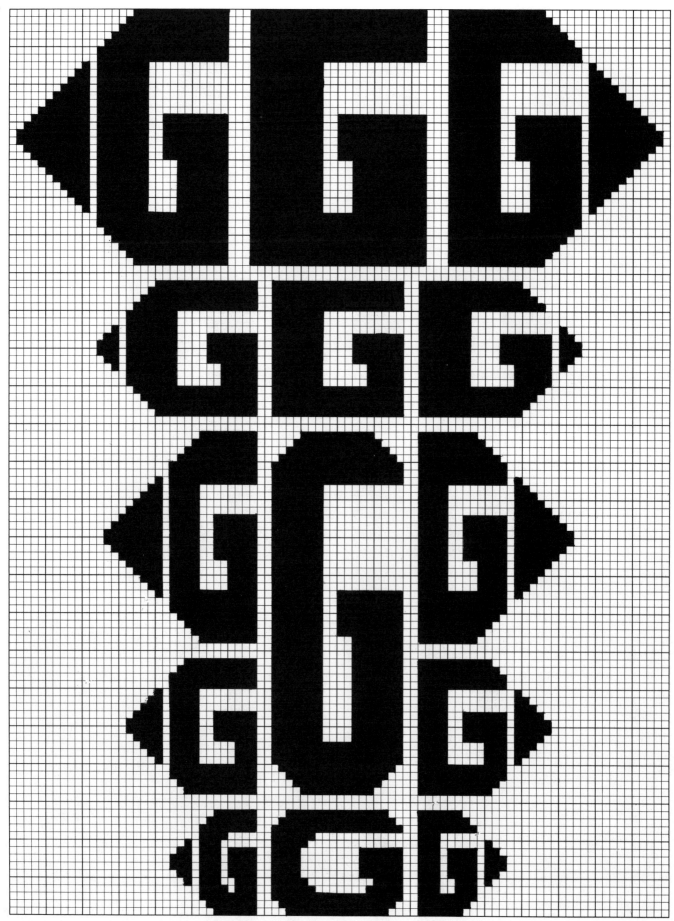

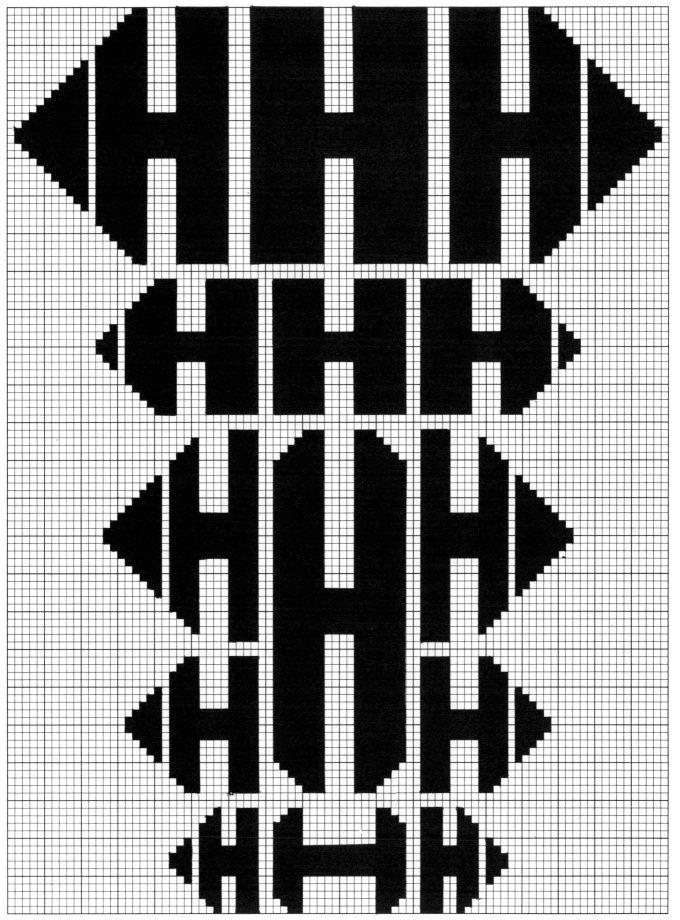

39

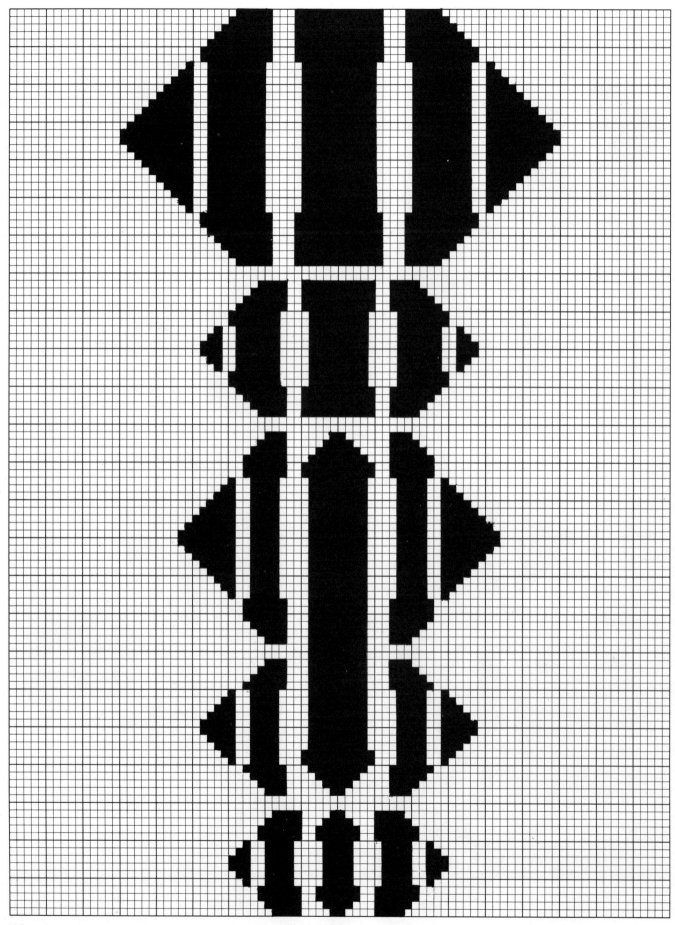

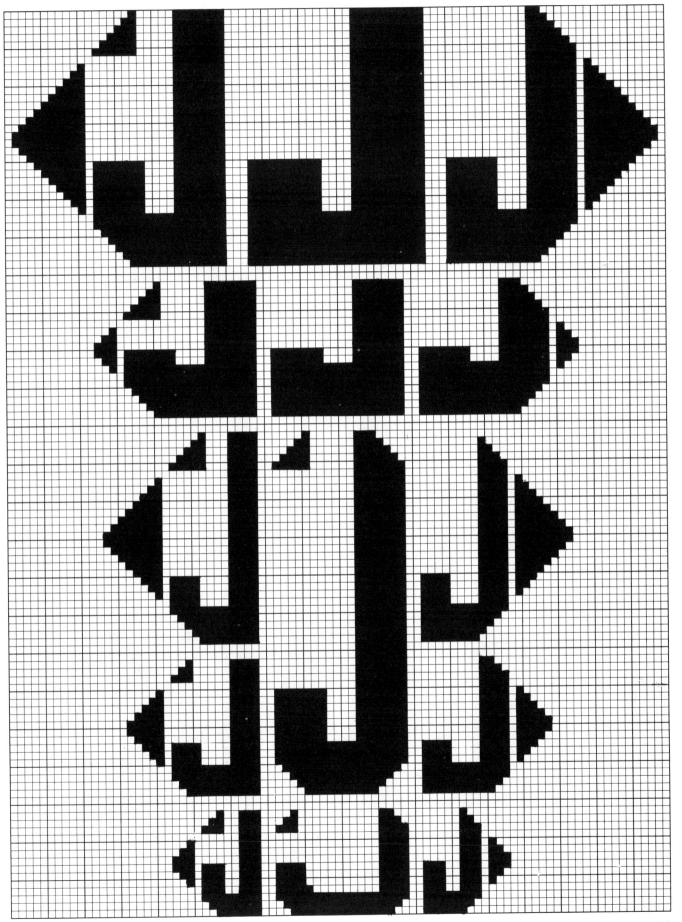

41

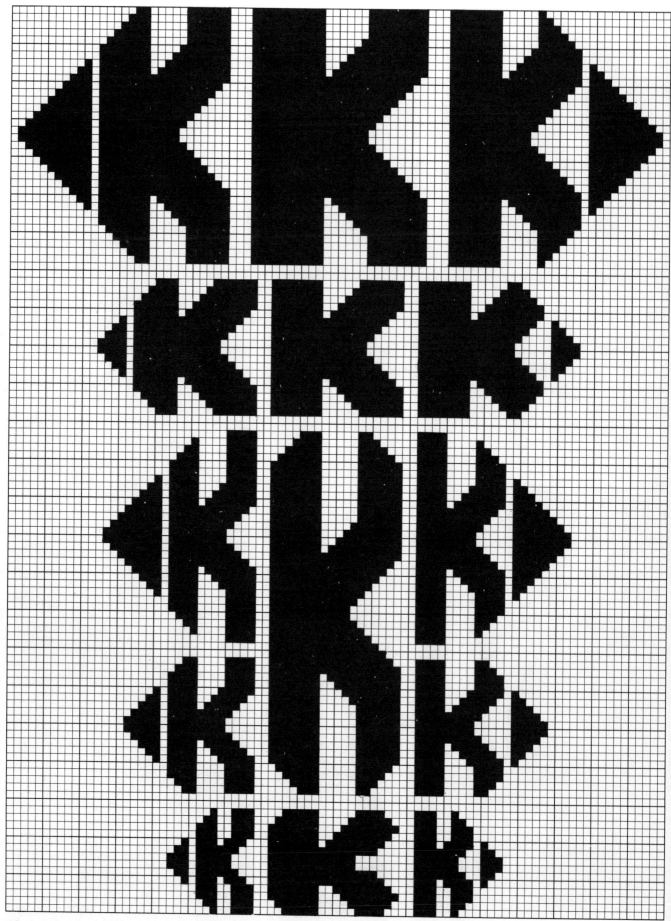

42

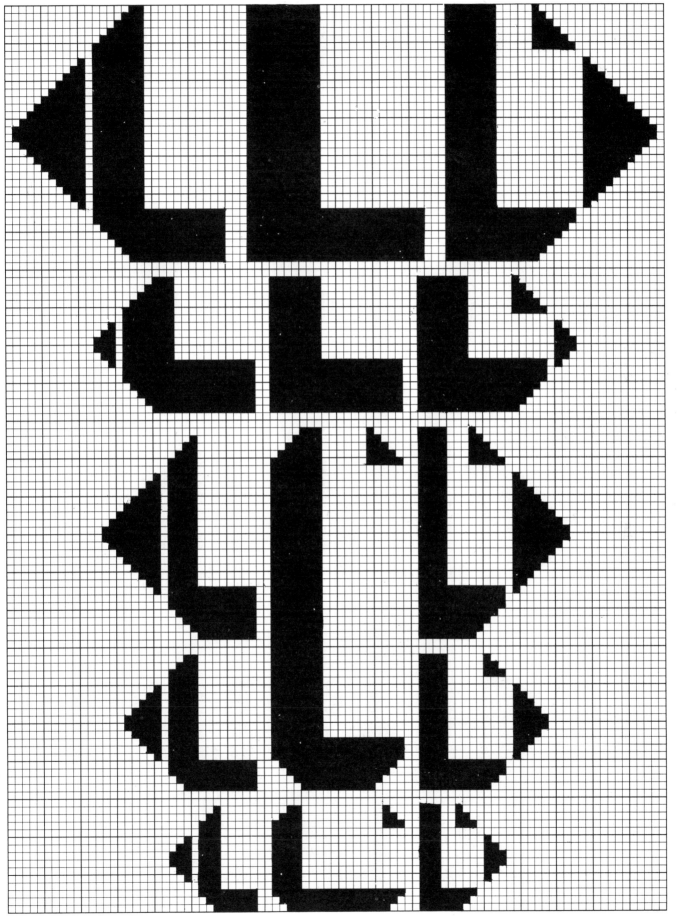

43

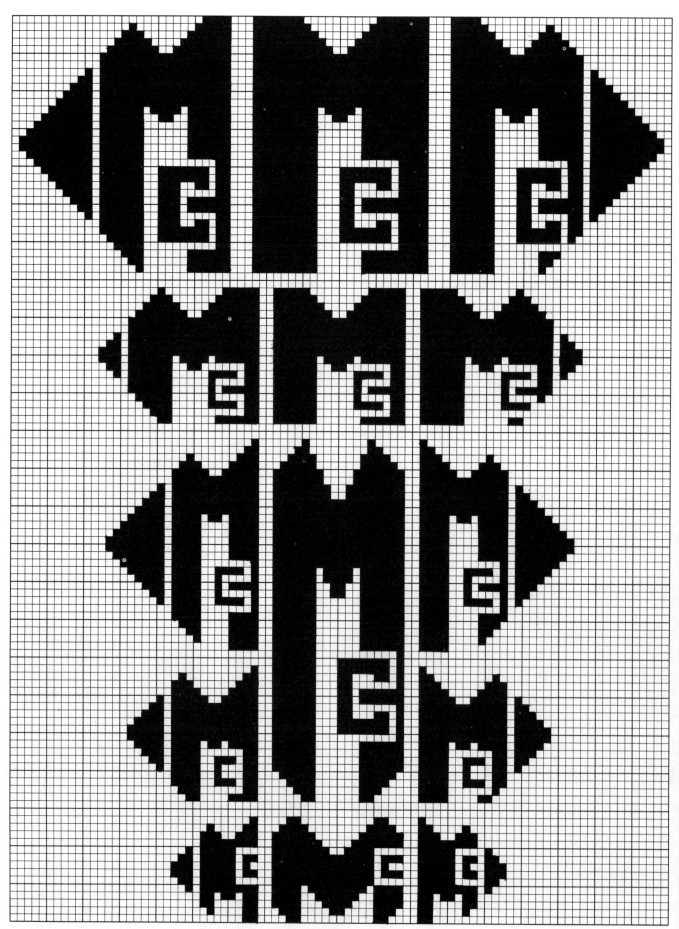

44

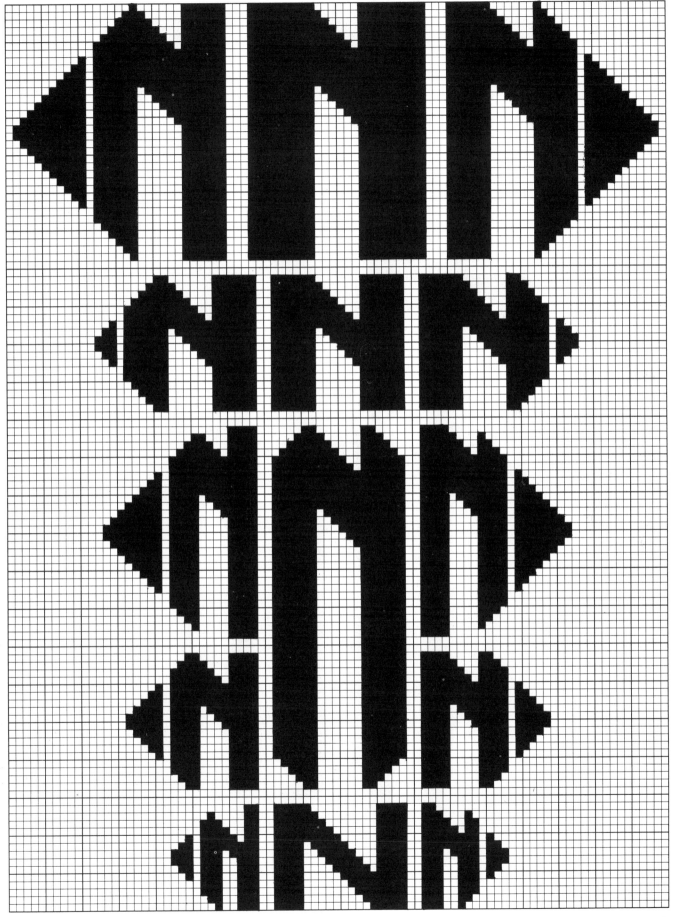

45

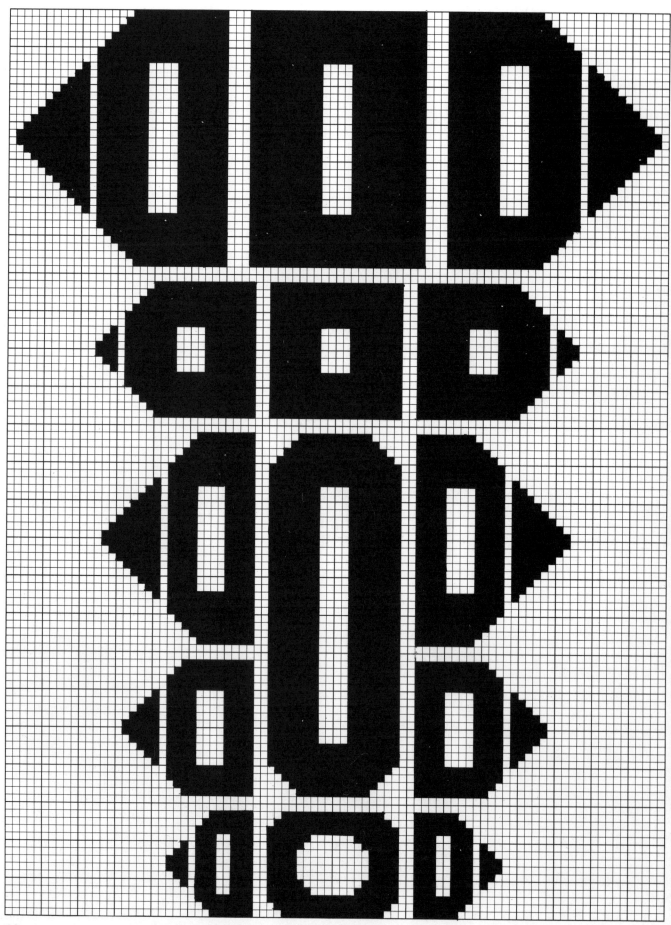

46

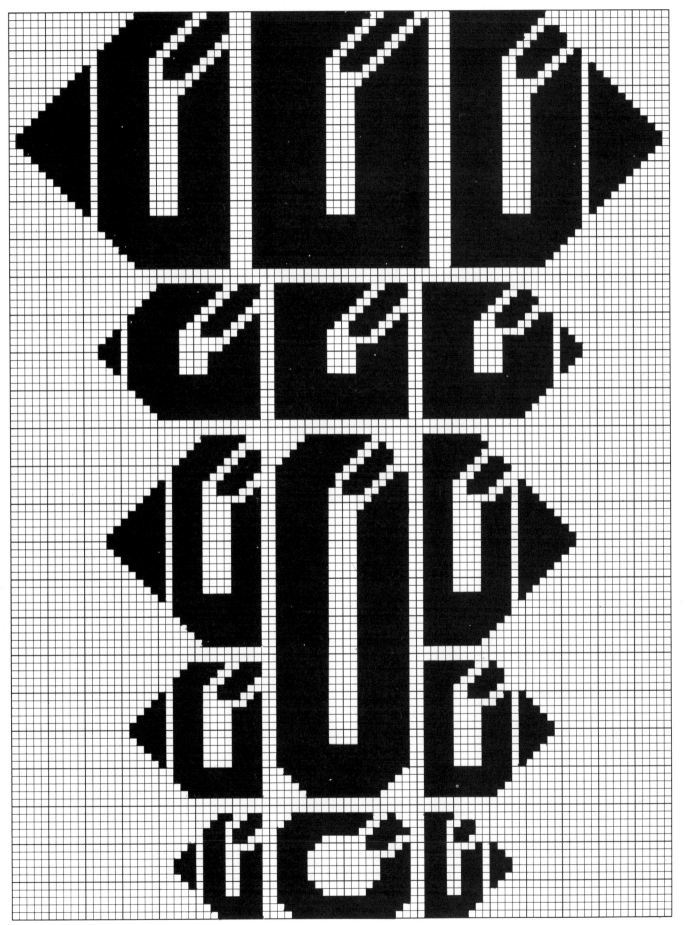

47

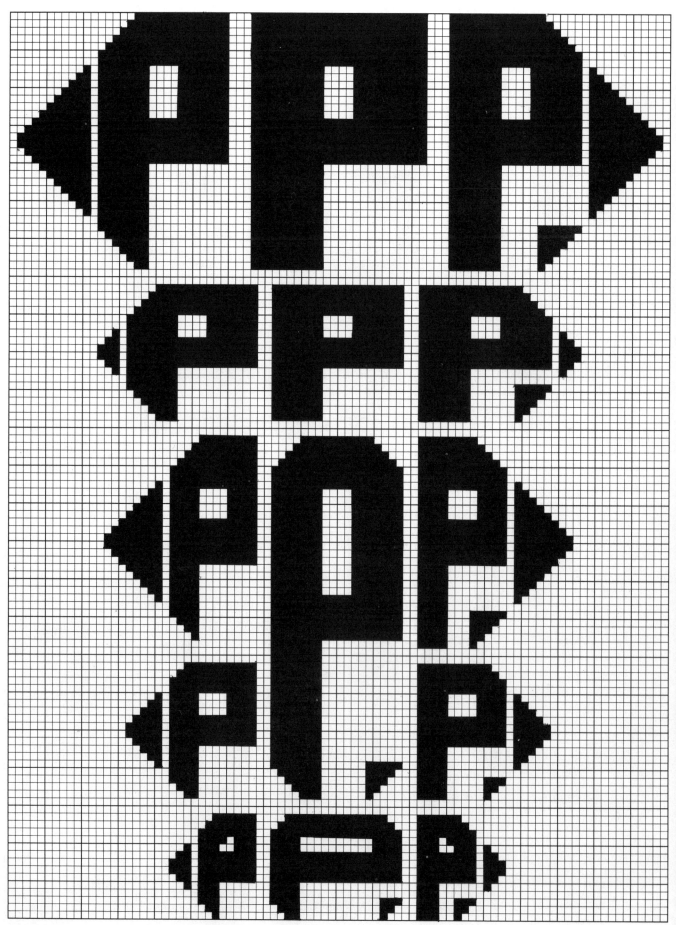

48

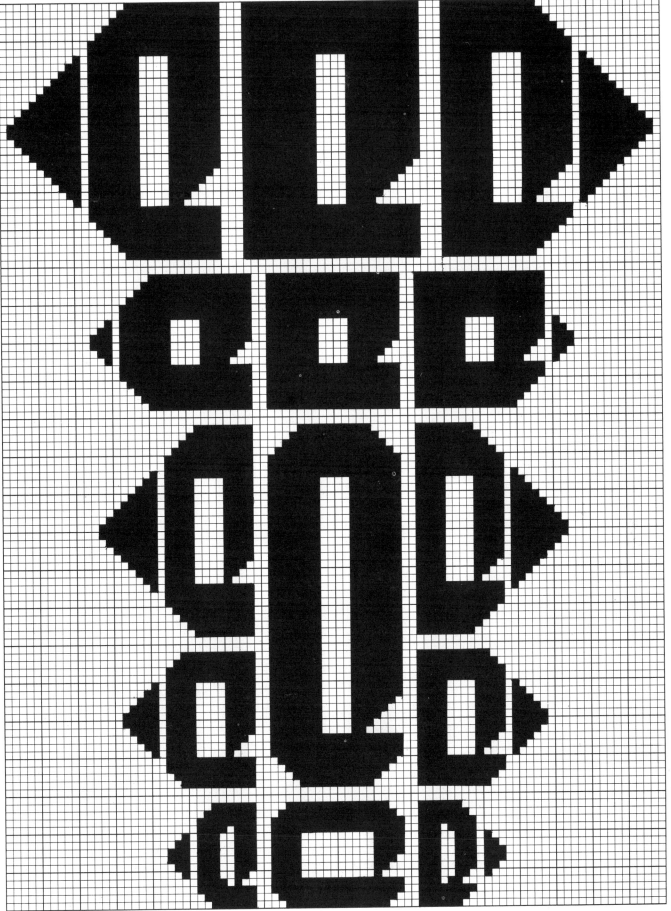

49

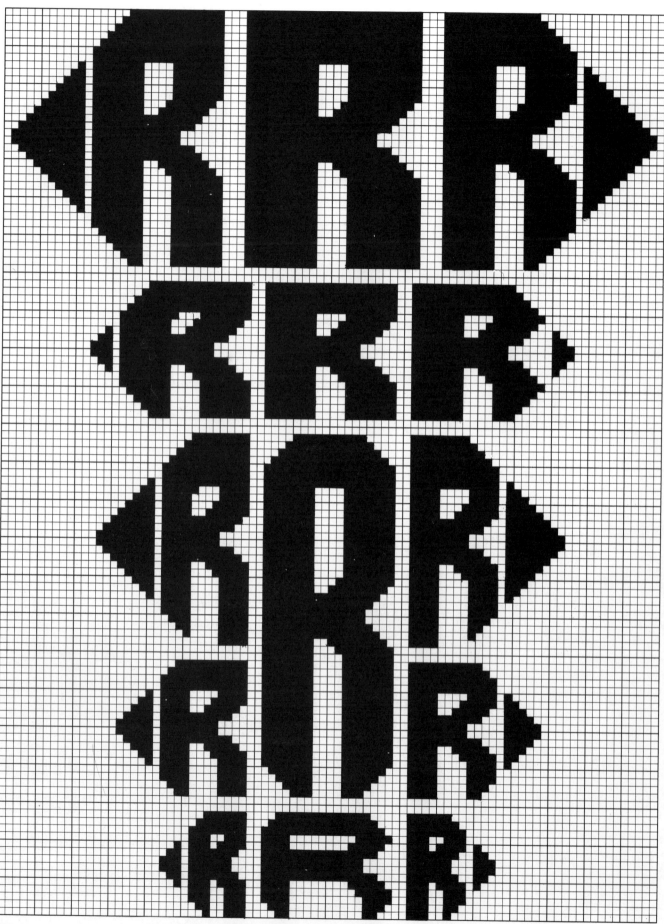

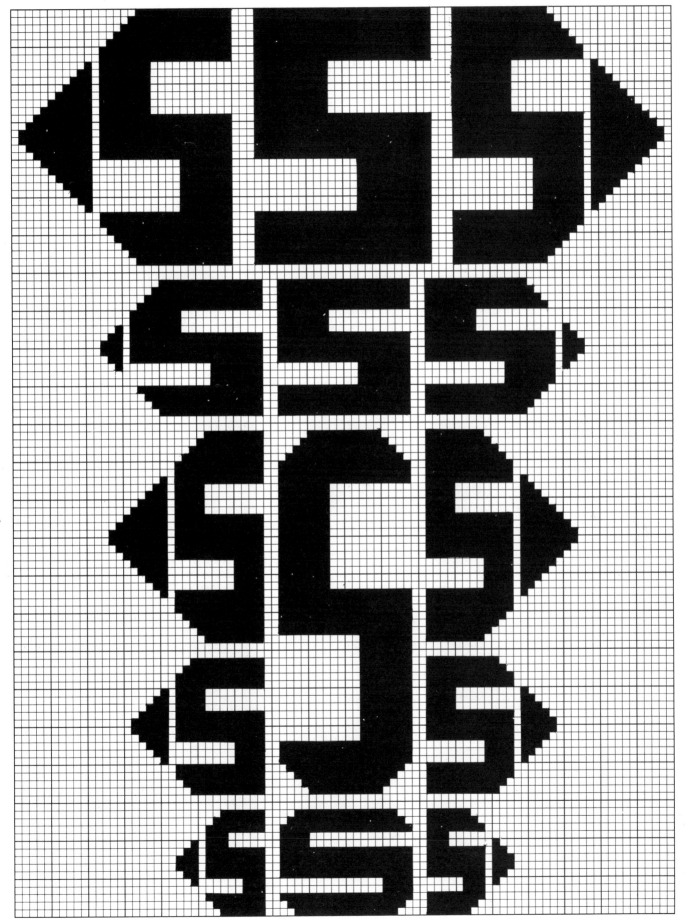

51

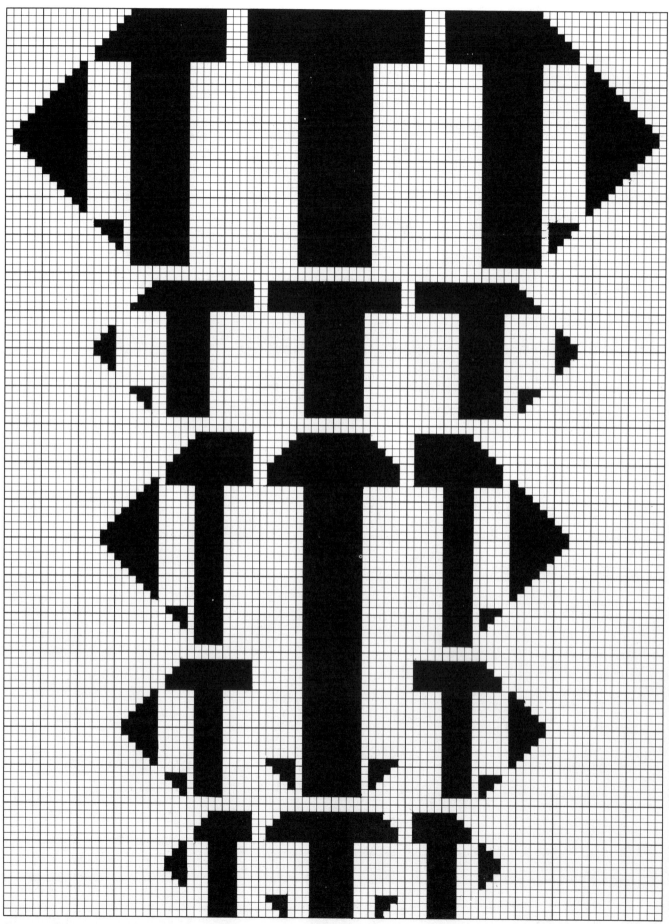

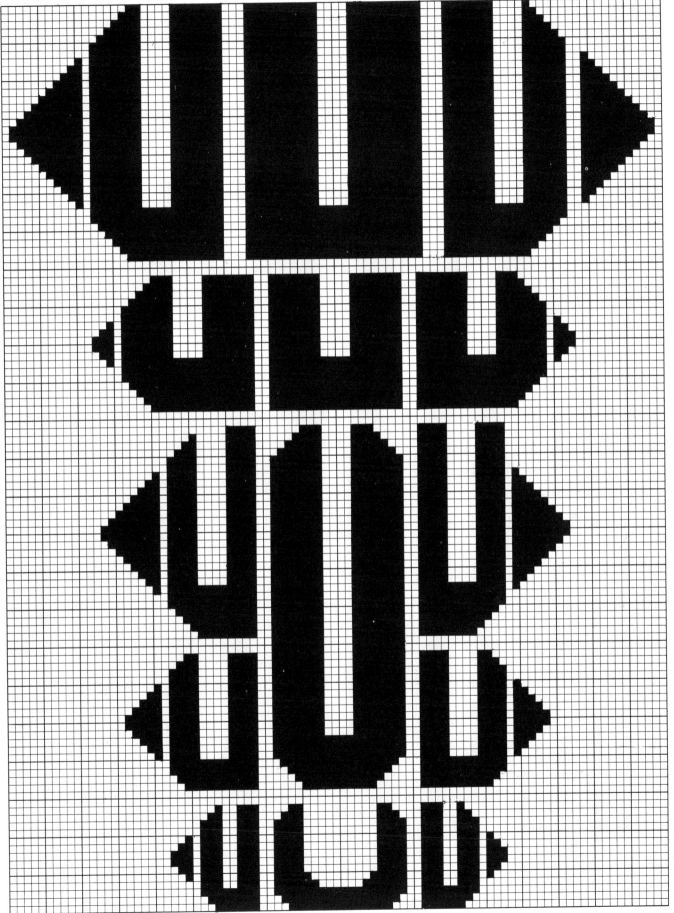

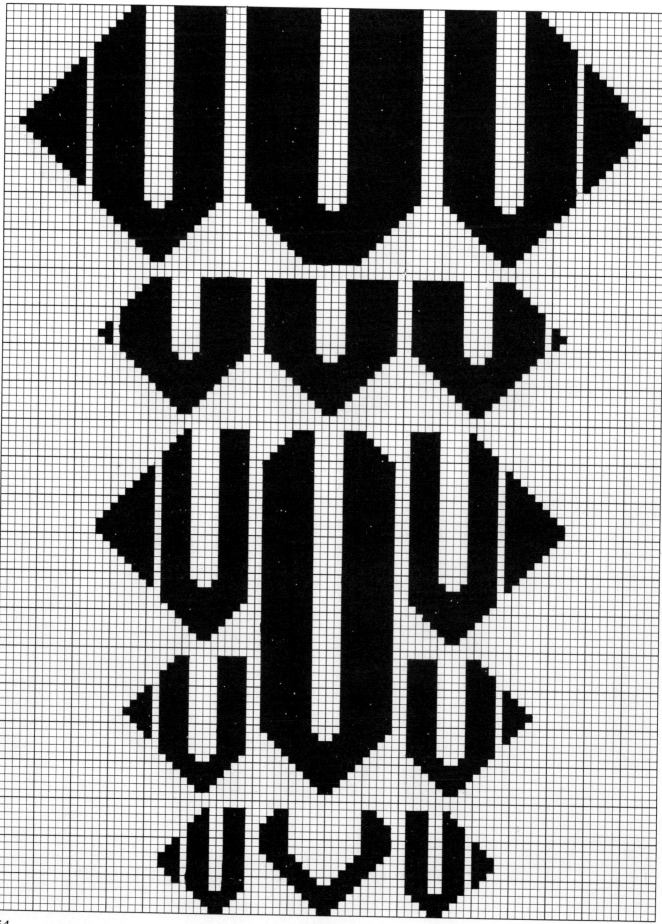

54

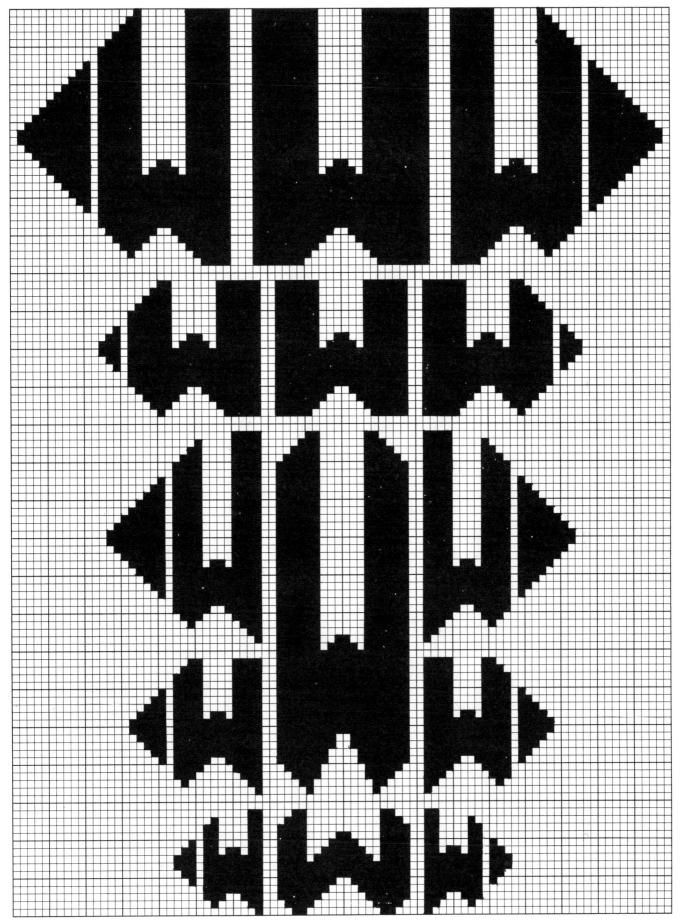

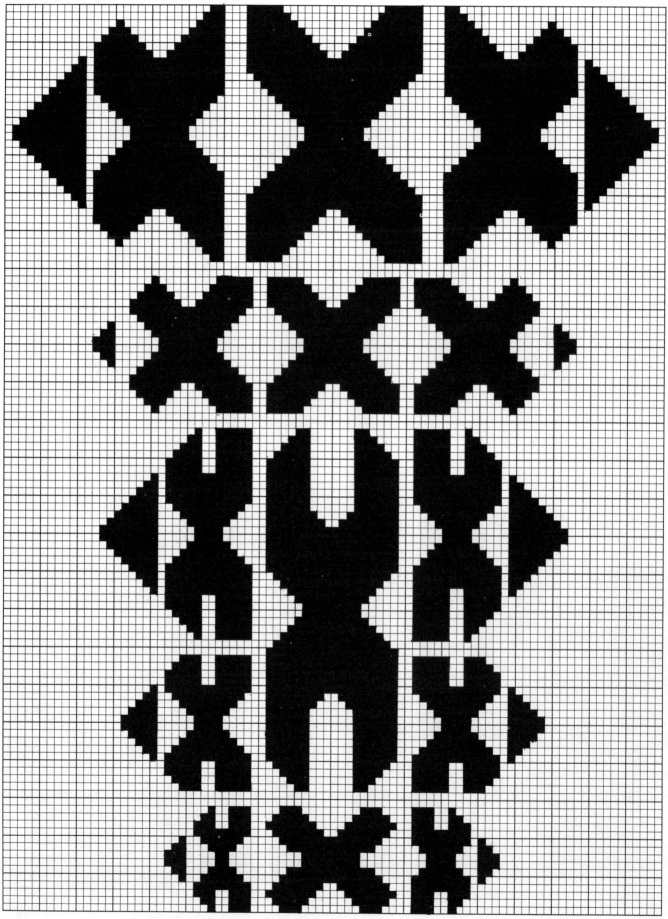

56

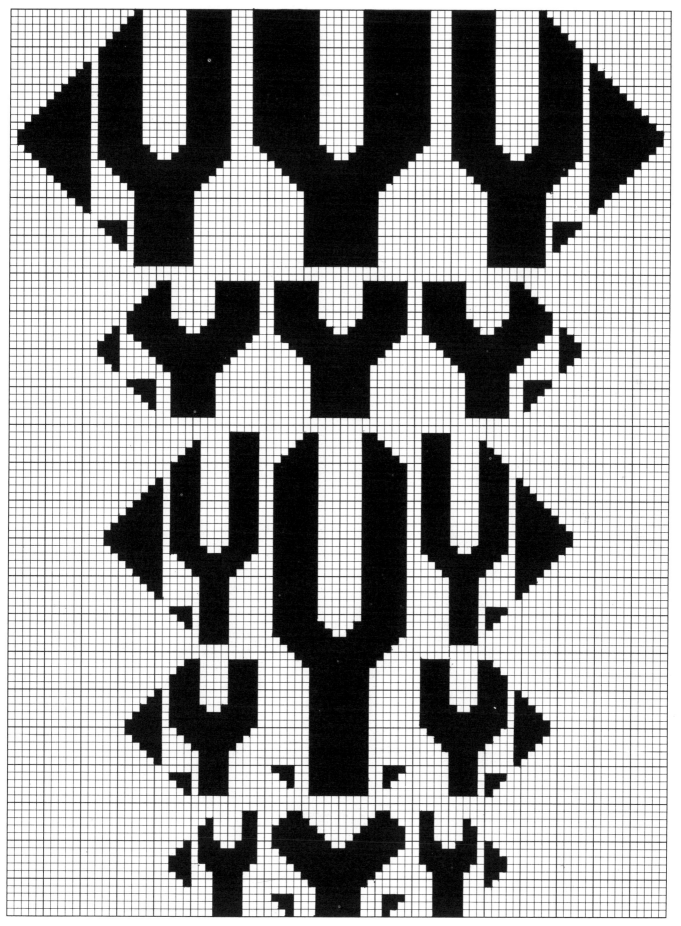

57

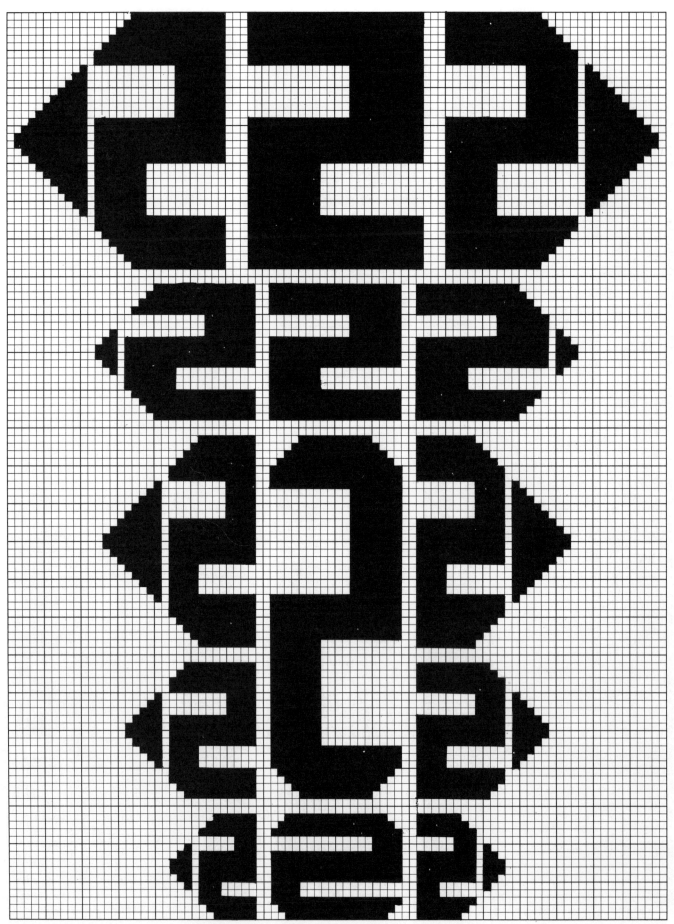

58

# Module 4    BIG AND BOLD

**F.J.N.**

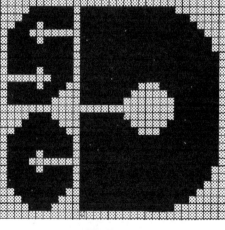

**F.J.G.**

**S.C.D.**

This style can fill many needs for letters that blend with contemporary decor while offering the needleworker challenging opportunities to experiment with color and texturing effects.

When designing with specific letters, unbalanced shapes placed next to, or overlapping, each other will suggest unique arrangements that would otherwise be difficult to anticipate or visualize. The *F. J. G.* design on this page is a case in point.

Four sizes of letters are given. Note that the smallest is one half as large as the queen-size, while the medium-size is one half as large as the king-size. These proportions make it easy to arrange three letters into a square. The *S.C.D.* design illustrates this concept.

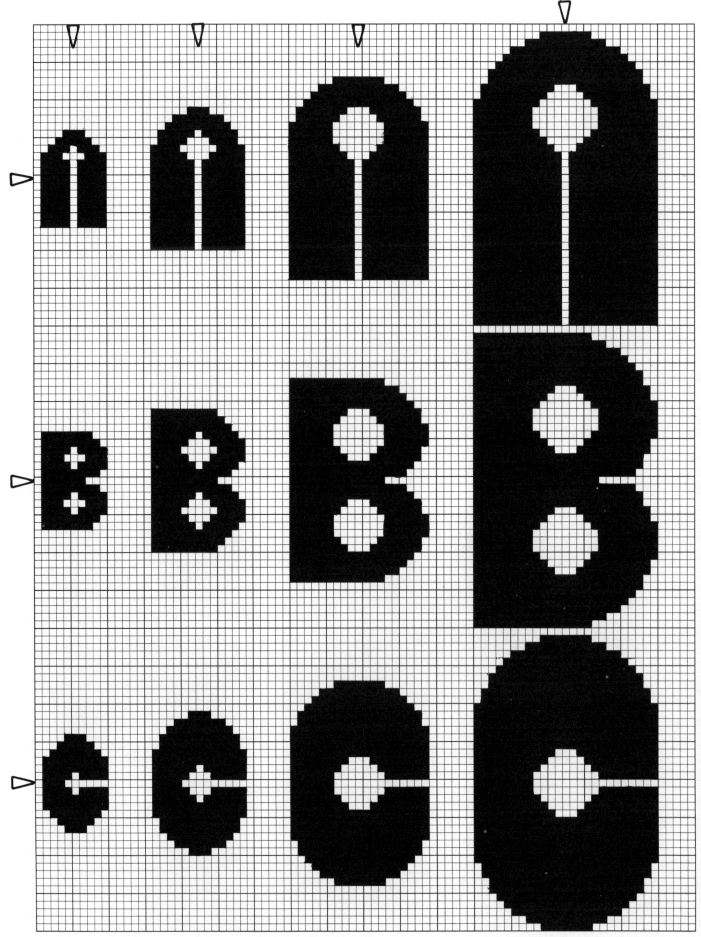

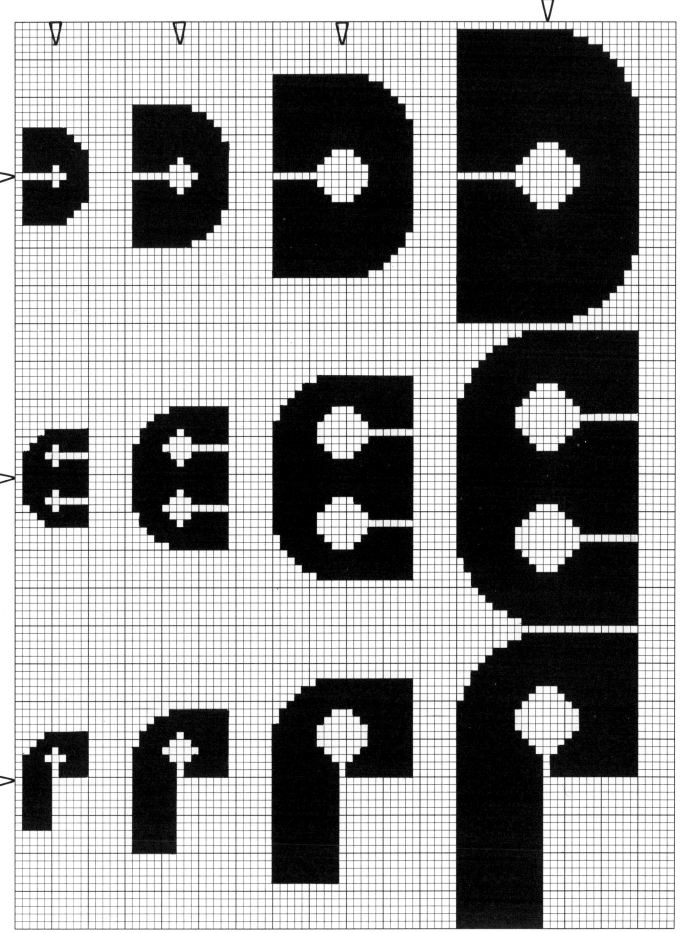

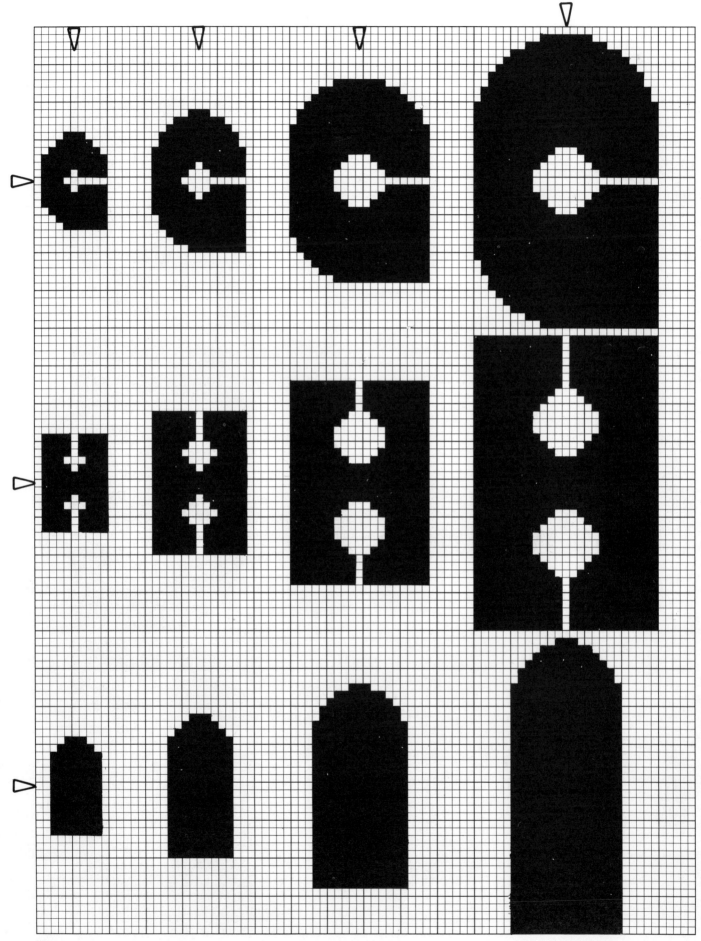

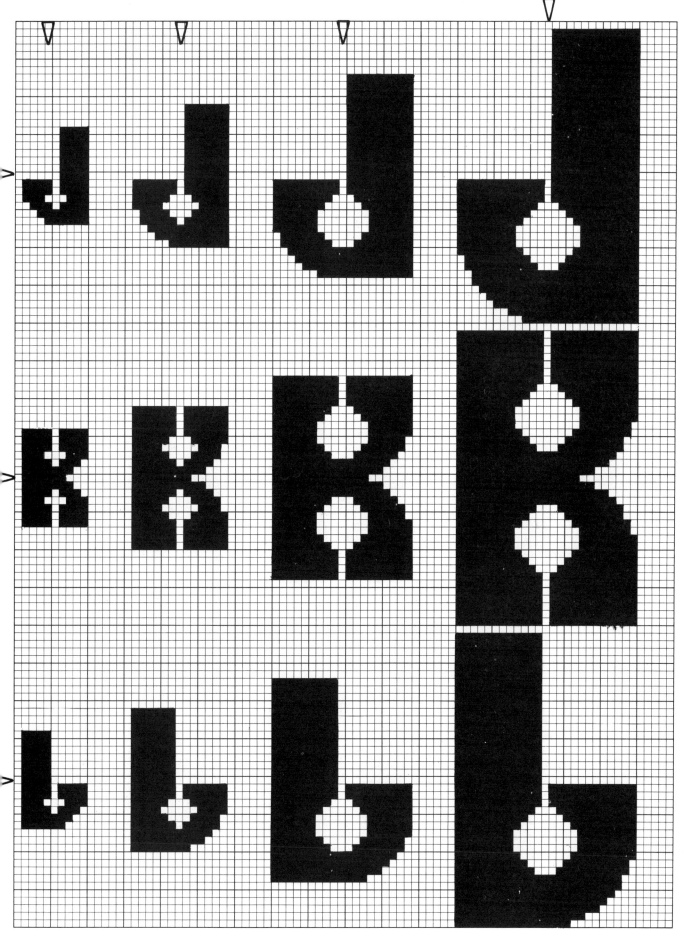

63

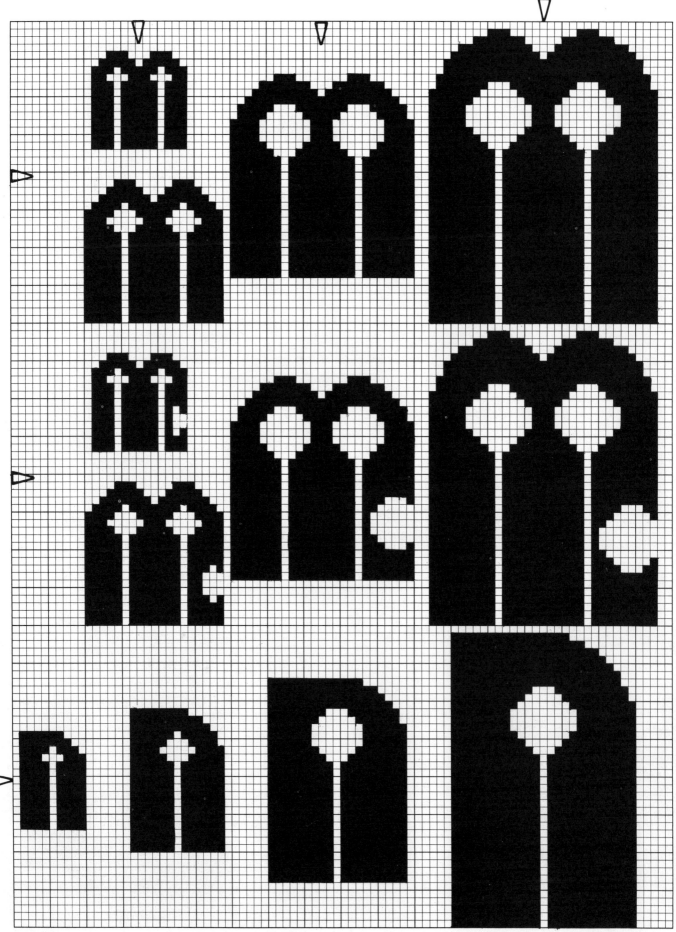

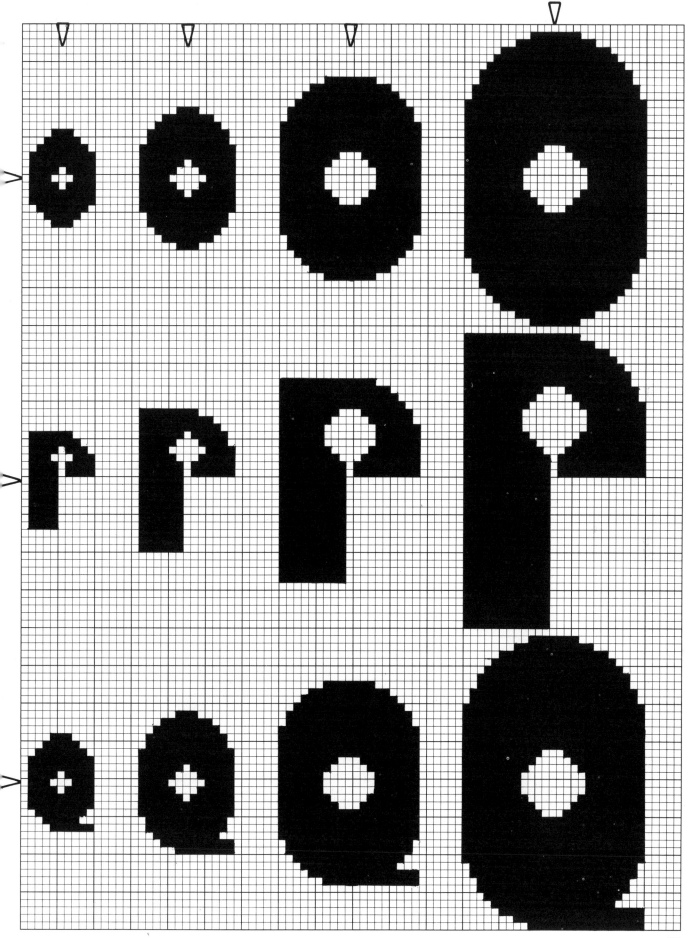

65

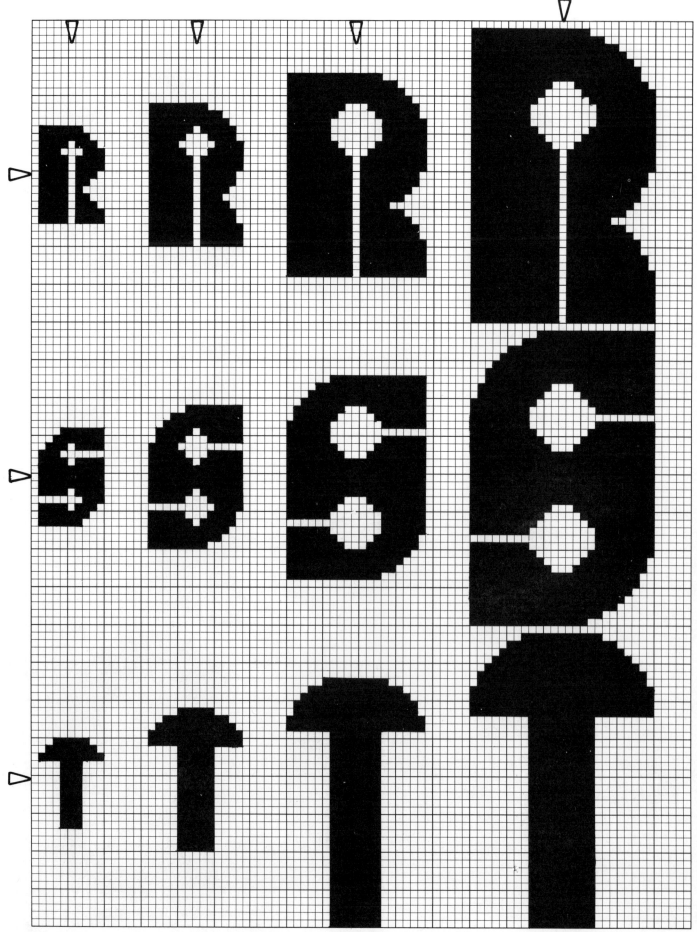

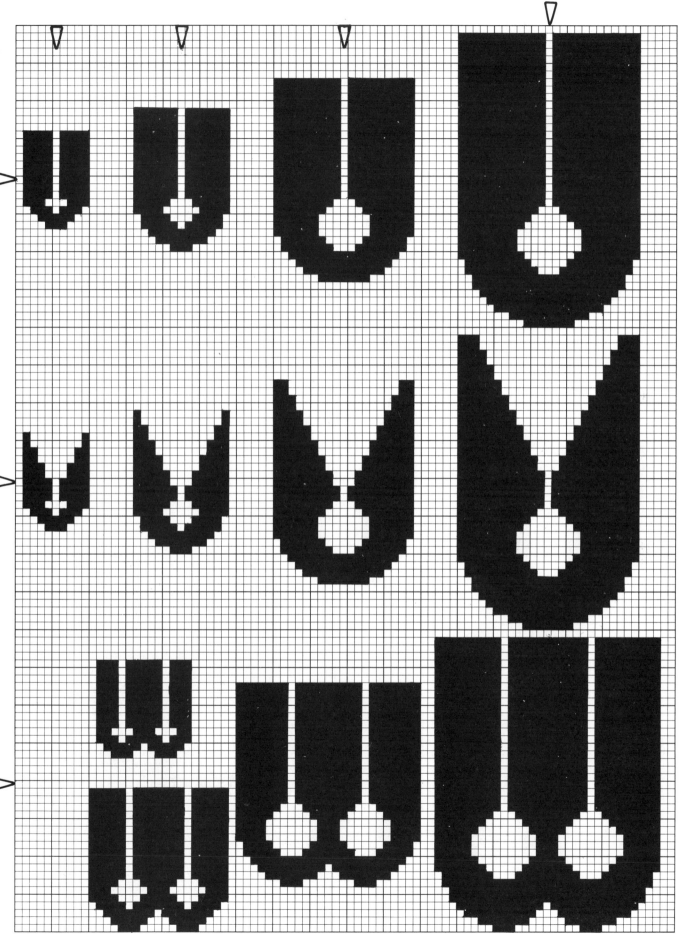

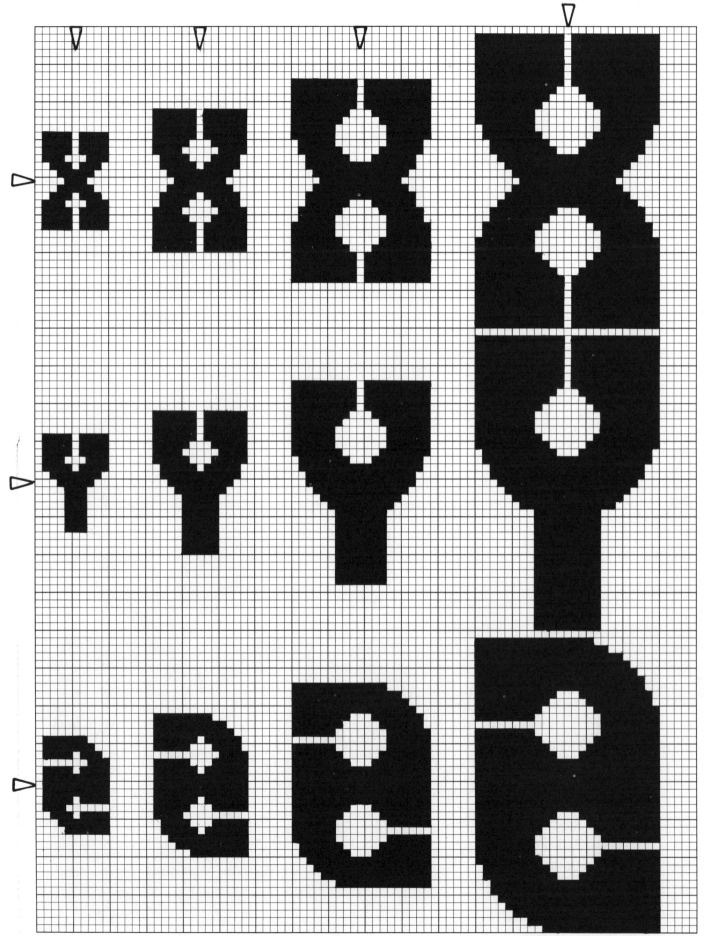

# Module 5    TRIANGLES

**K.R.D.**

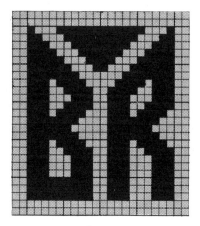

**B.R.**

**F.J.N.**

**B.R.**

You will be able to arrange the letters of this module in more ways than seem possible at first glance. Consider units of the same size lined up like soldiers on parade, as suggested in the sample pages; put letters into rectangular boxes or vertical lines; experiment with nested, overlapped, or intertwined arrangements.

The letters here may also be used with some of the SQUARES AND RECTANGLES alphabets, and with the smaller letters in the DIAMOND Module.

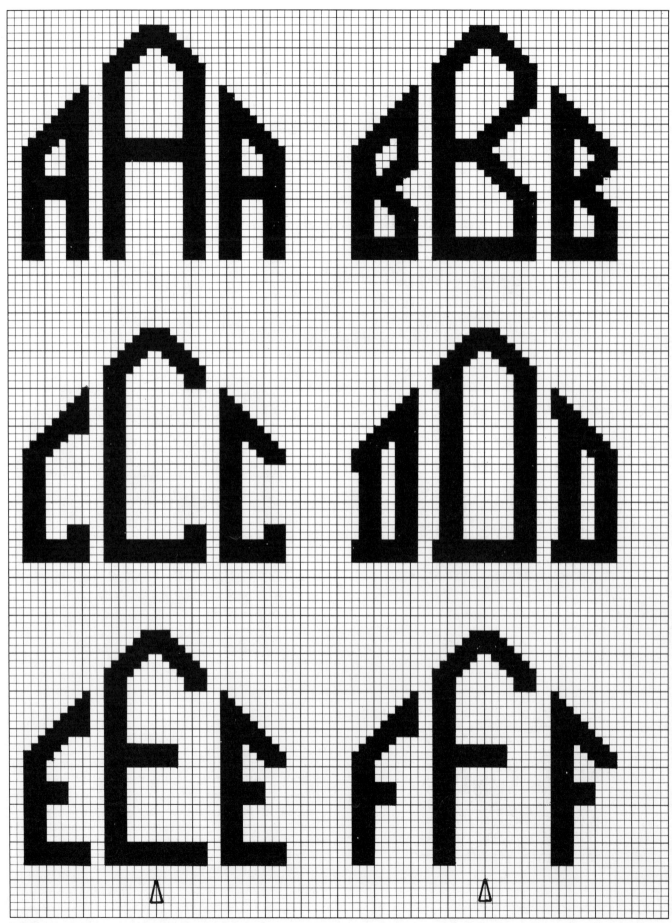

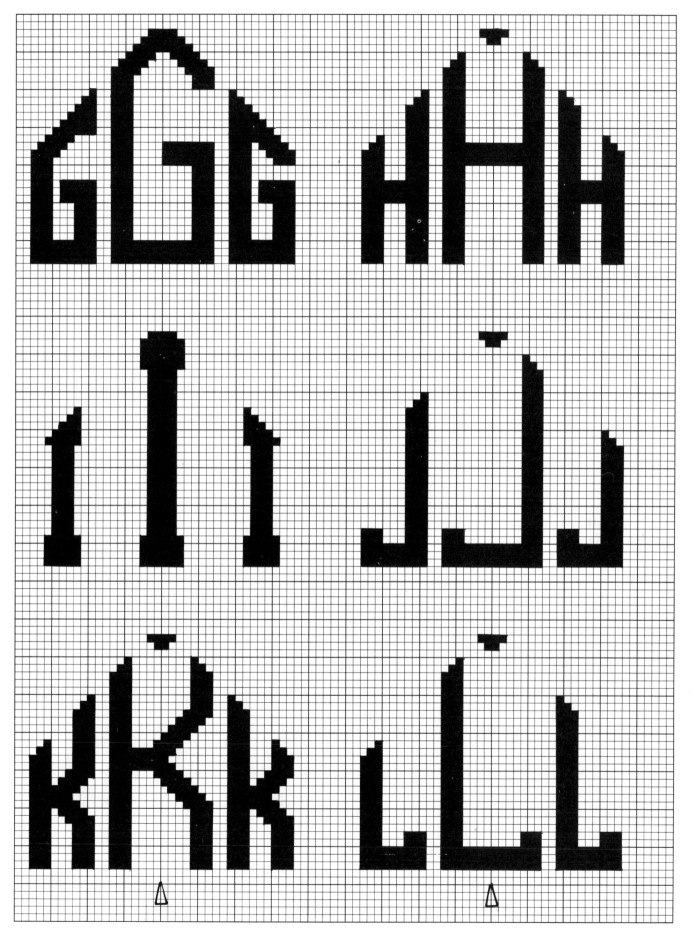

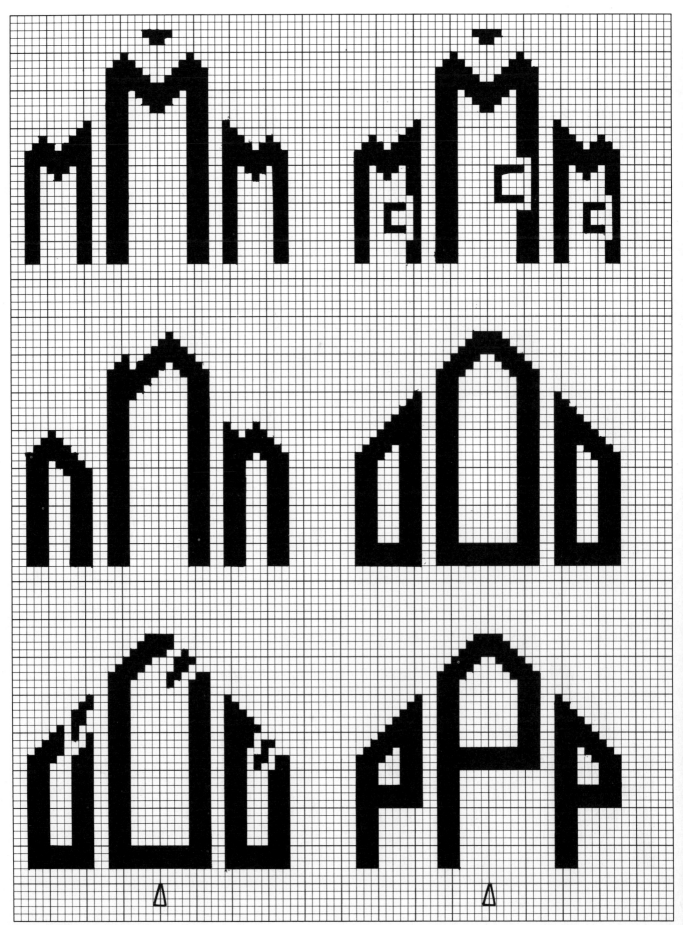

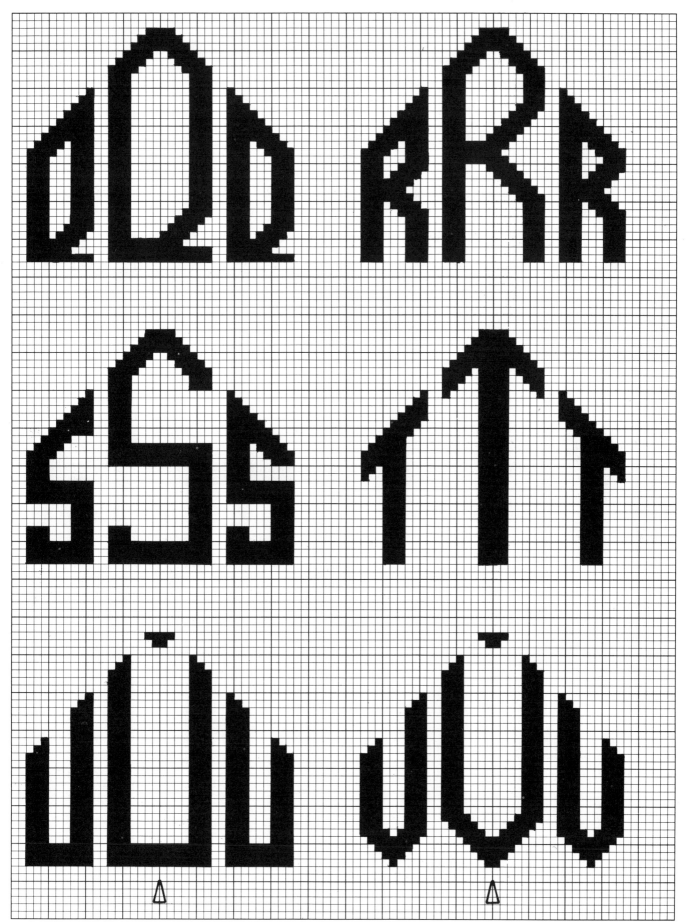

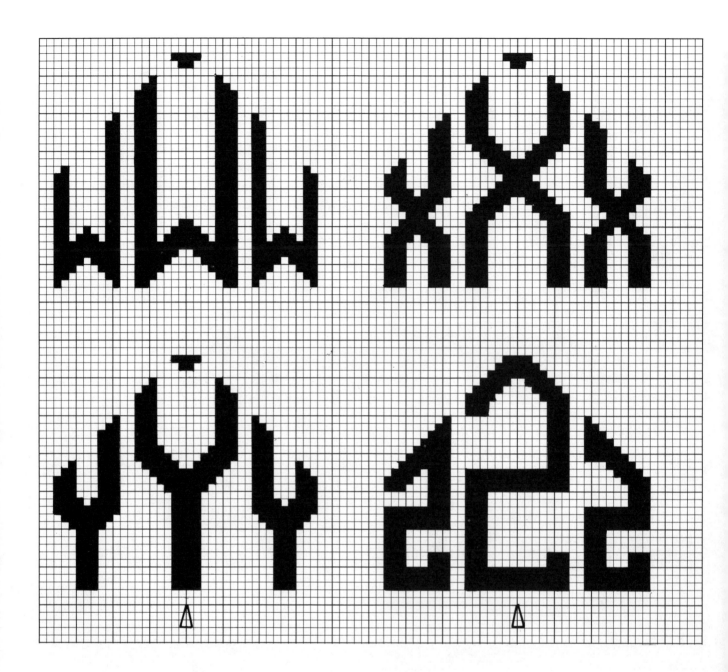

# Module 6    DIAMONDS

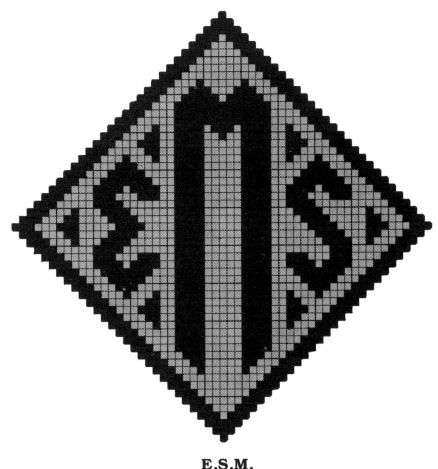

**E.S.M.**

This module uses vertical and diagonal lines only. The 45-degree angle contributes to the symmetry of each letter and thereby to the good balance of any arrangement in which these letters are used.

The small triangle and diamond motifs in the graphs are aids for the centering and counting processes. They also help solidify the diamond-shaped contour, but you may want to eliminate them if you put a frame around your design. A frame will enlarge the overall dimensions of your design while providing an enclosed area in which to use another background color and stitch pattern. If framing is desired, a simple line border such as the one used here, a geometric motif forming a band, or even ornate scrolling will all be appropriate with these aristocratic-looking letter forms.

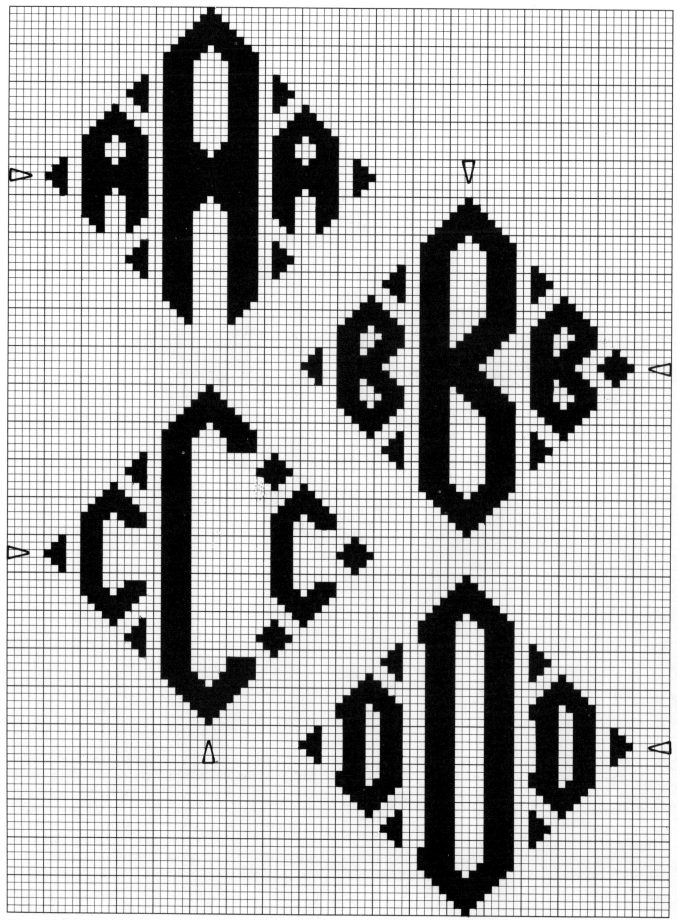

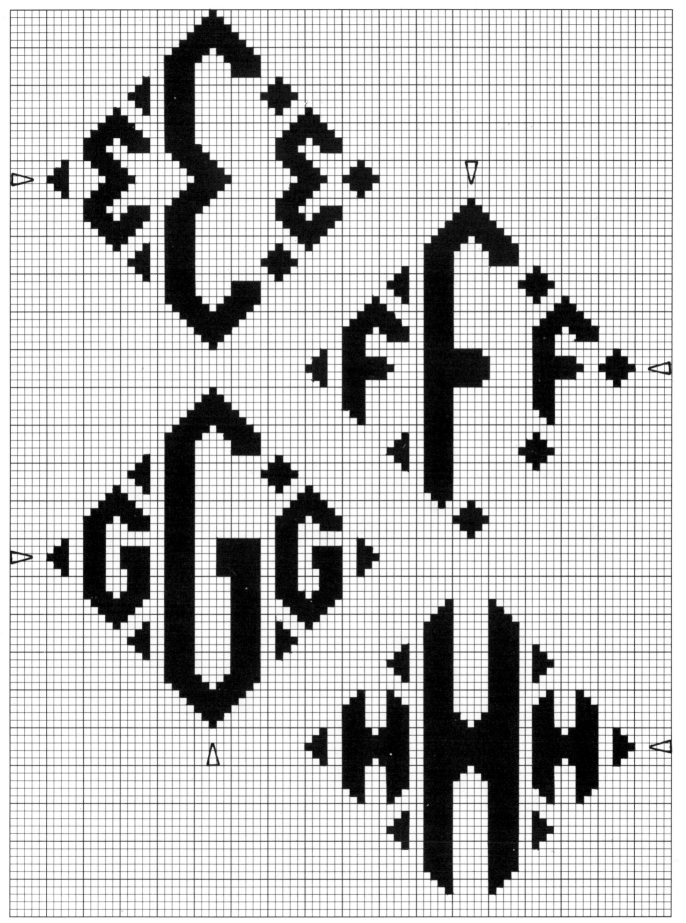

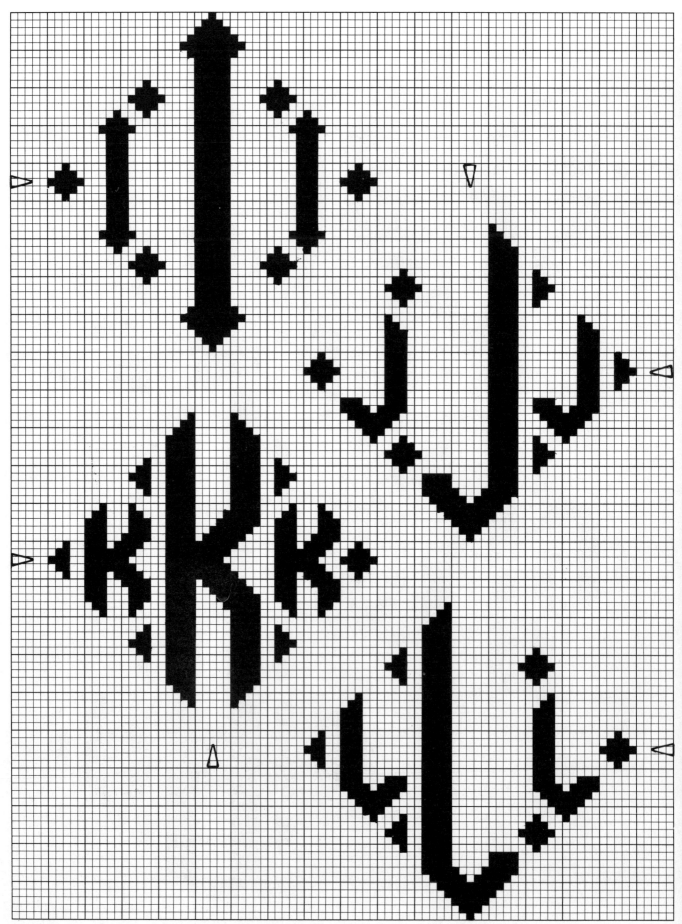

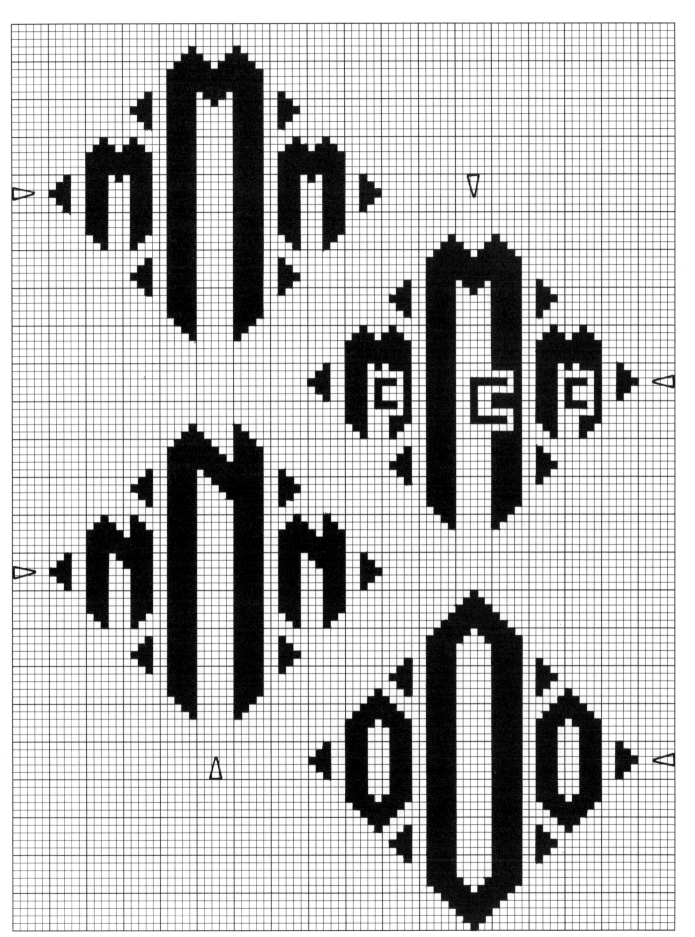

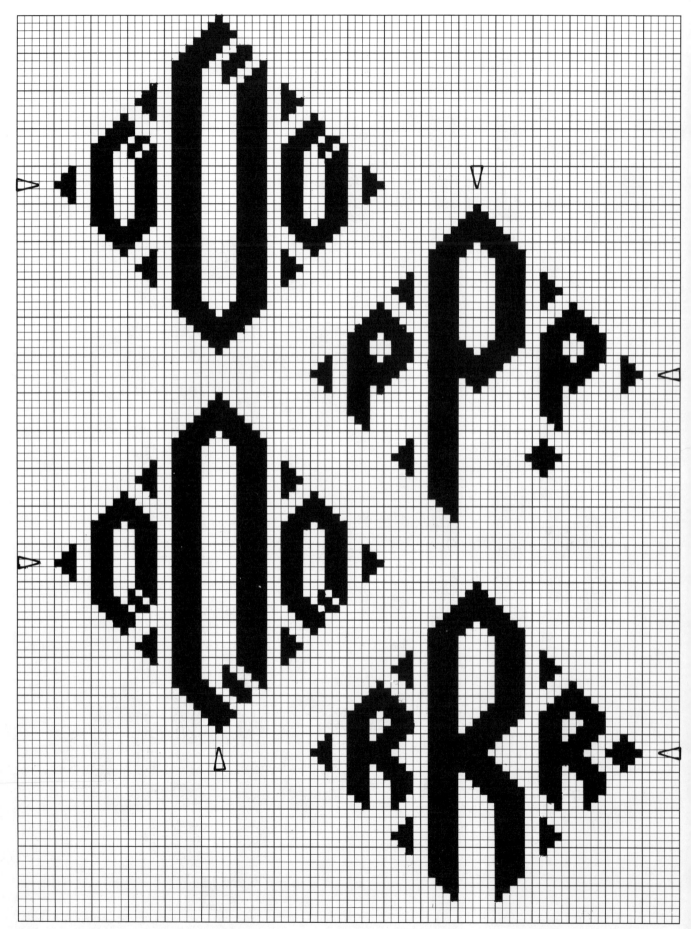

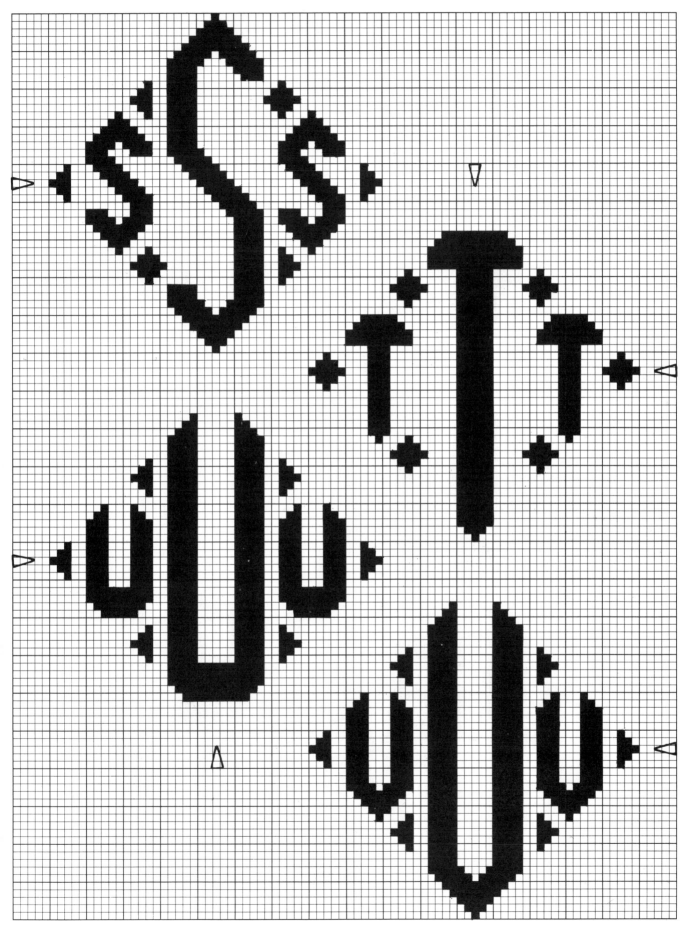

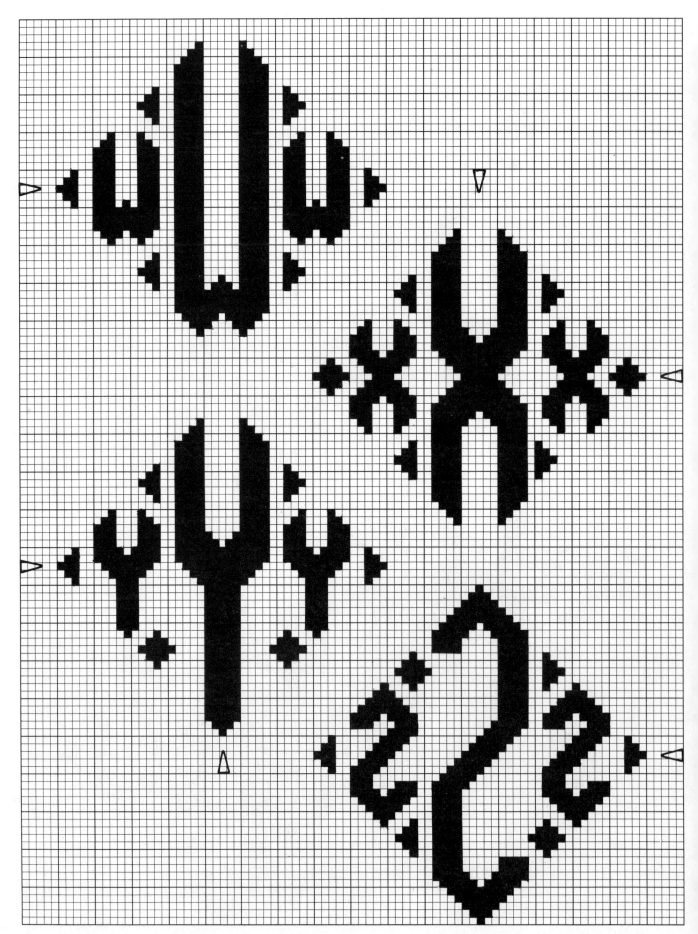

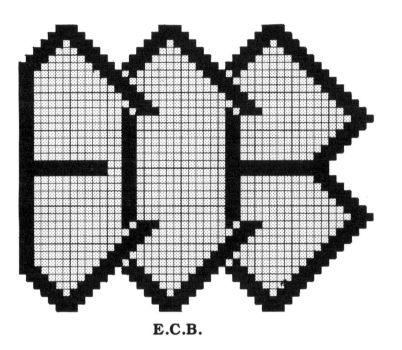

E.C.B.

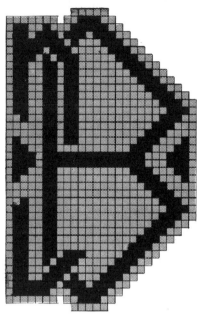

N.L.B.

C.H.G.

G.S.

This is one of the most versatile of the 13 modules in this book. The easiest and most successful way to design with these letters is with the help of plain tracing paper. Make rough tracings of several sizes and styles of each of the needed letters on separate pieces of paper. Overlay your tracings and shift the component letters to suggest unusual arrangements. Overlap letters, move them up and down, dovetail them, reverse letters, intertwine the angular and vertical styles. When you have a design you like, you can then work it out more carefully on graph paper.

If your final choice of design features an over-under lacing effect, refer to the introduction for ways to execute it.

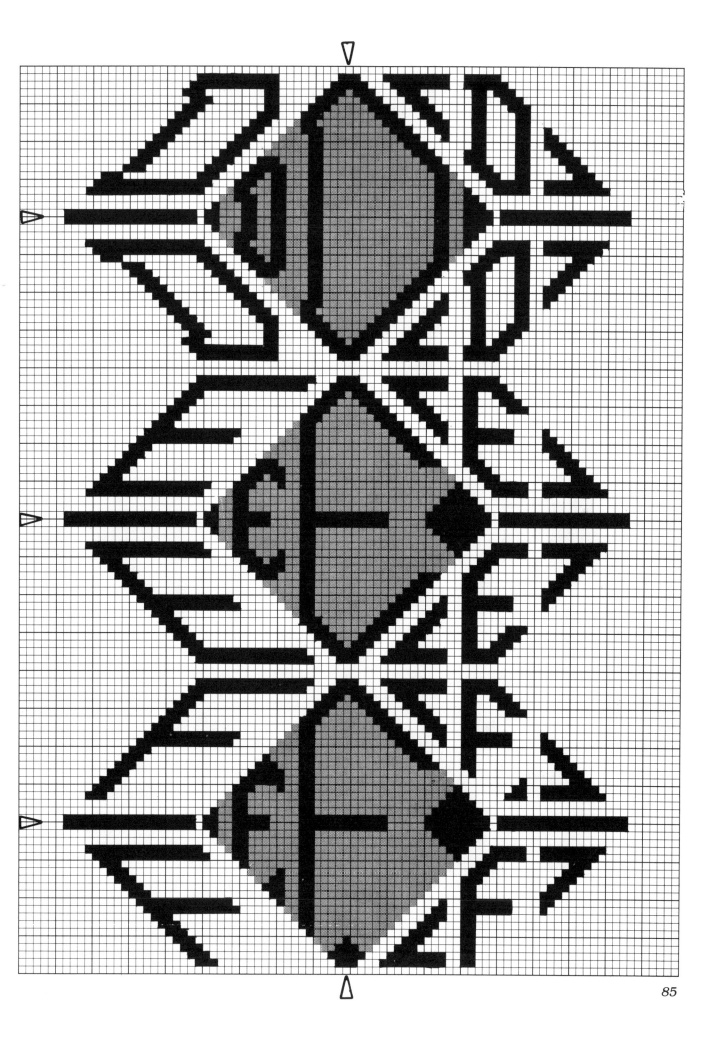

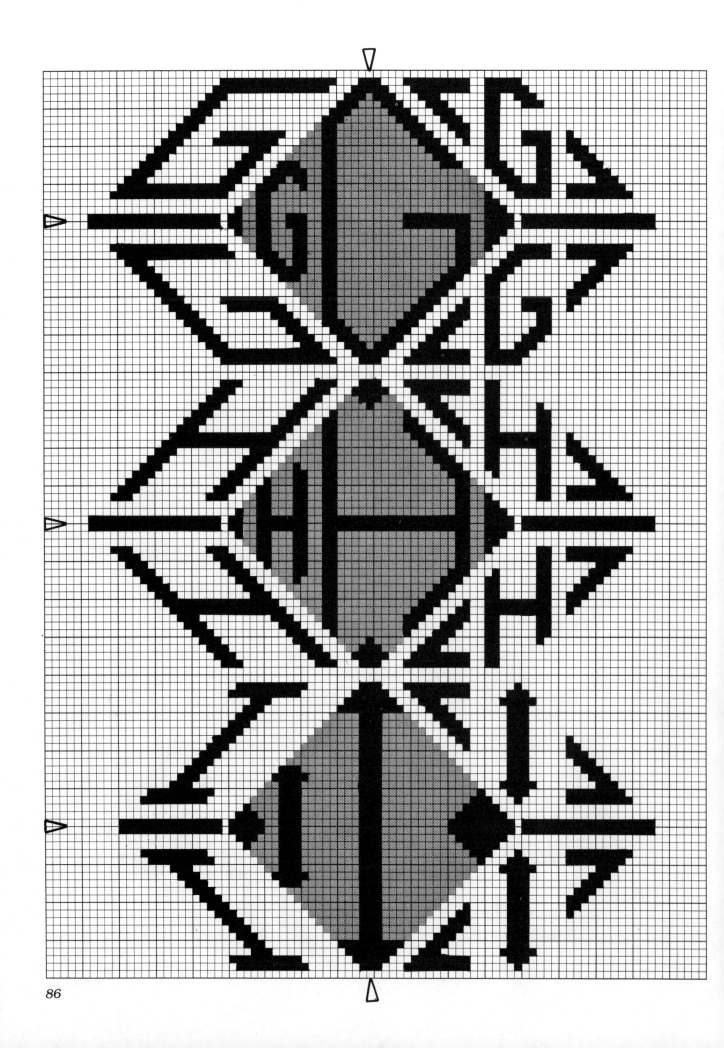

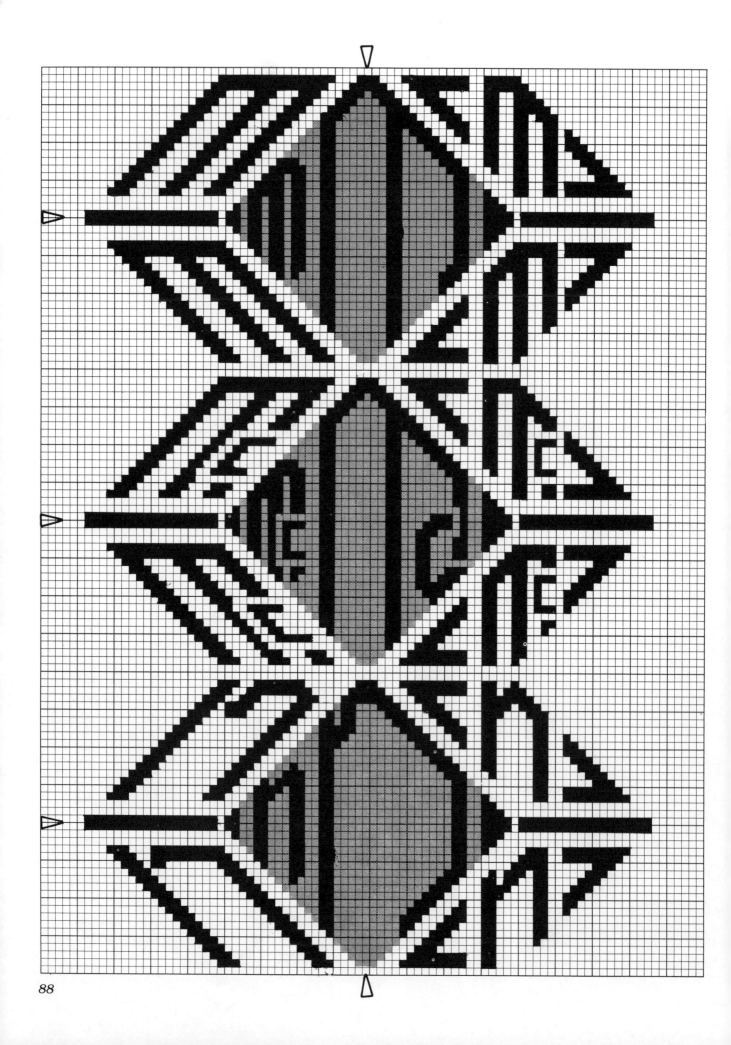

89

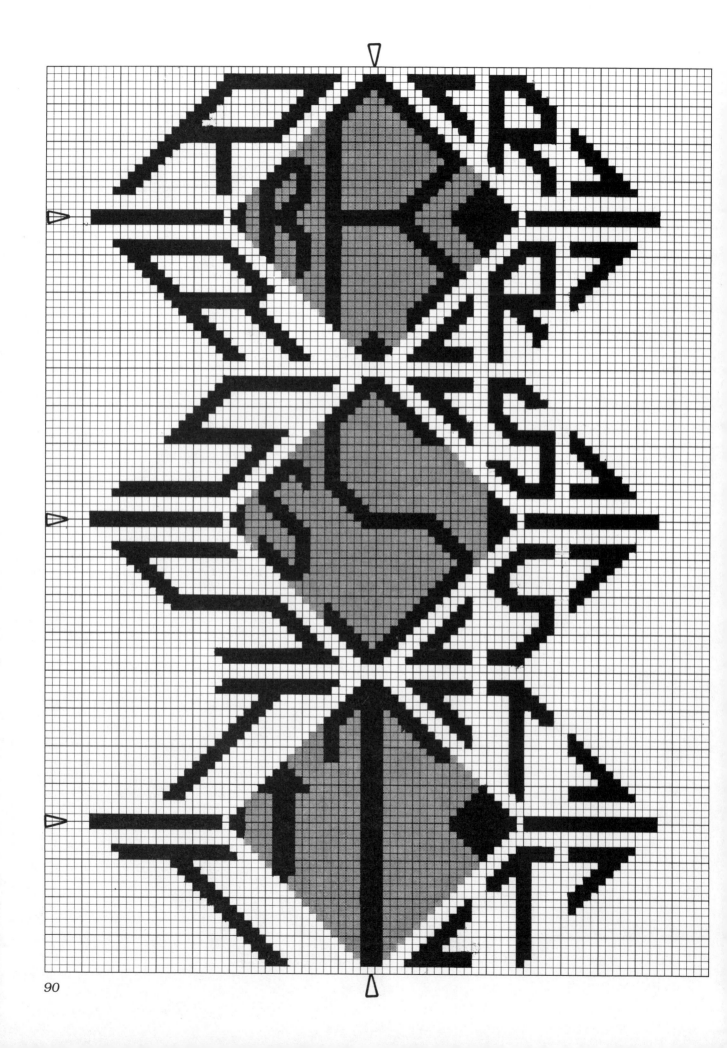

91

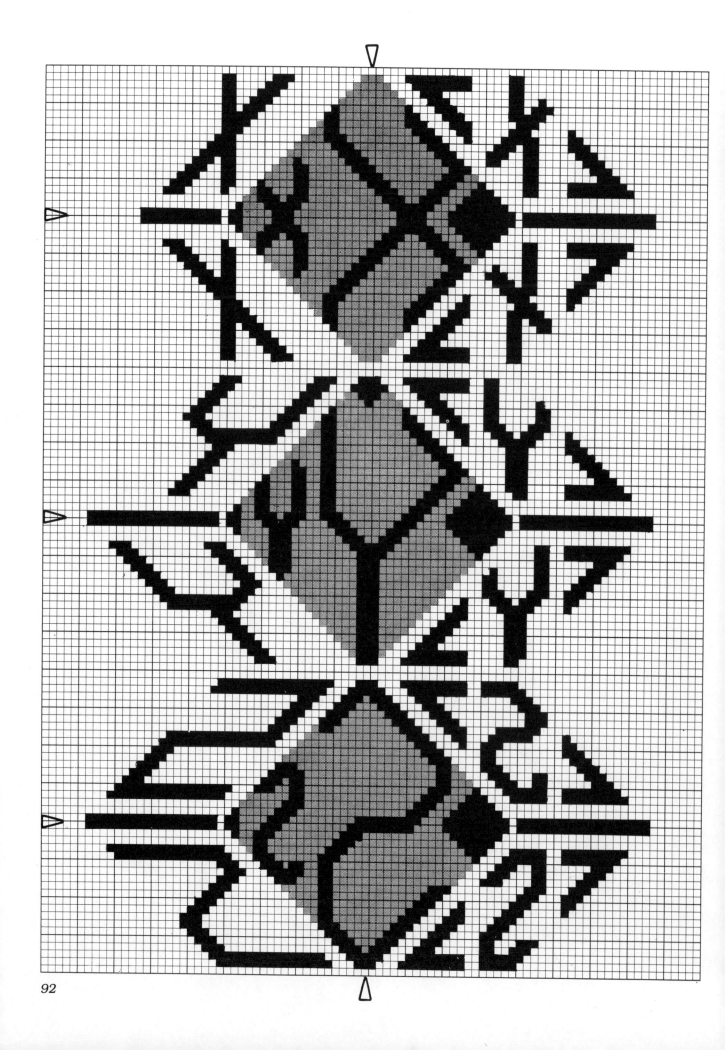

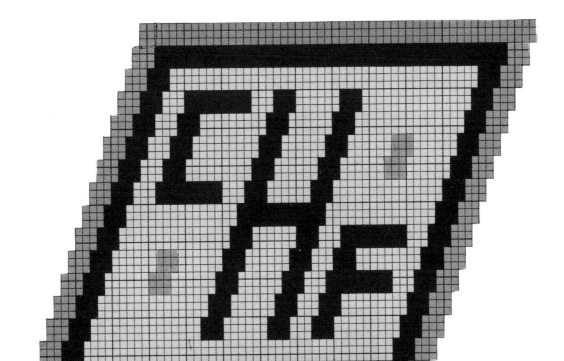

**C.F.H.**

**D.S.**

You can rescale the letters of this module to almost any size you need; you can also execute them in a wide variety of stitches and texturing effects.

The unit of design that makes up each letter is a square. A three-mesh square is used for each of the two alphabets here, but any size square may be substituted. The *D.S.* monogram is an example of substitution by a five-mesh square unit. Larger units will increase overall size while decreasing the angle of incline.

Horizontal or Vertical Gobelin may, of course, be used for any size unit, but suggested diagonal stitch patterns for three-mesh square units are Tent, Cross, Italian or Braided Cross, Scotch, Tied Scotch, or Cross Scotch.

A few suggestions for four-square units are Rice or Giant Rice, Mosaic, Smyrna Cross, Oblong or Giant Tied Cross, or Divided Scotch.

Rescaling to even larger units multiplies the number of pattern possibilities, which become too numerous to list here.

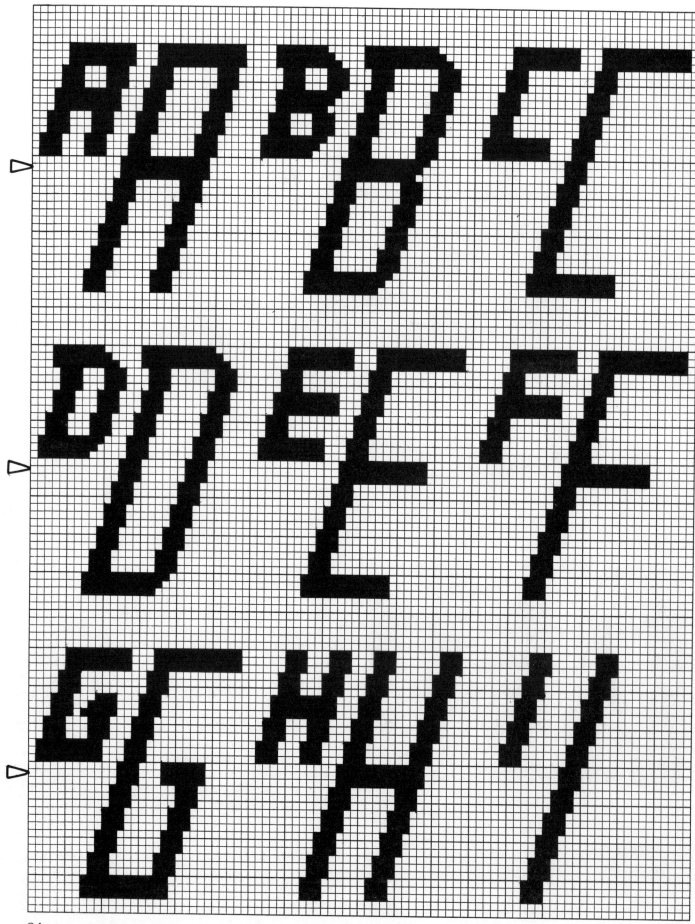

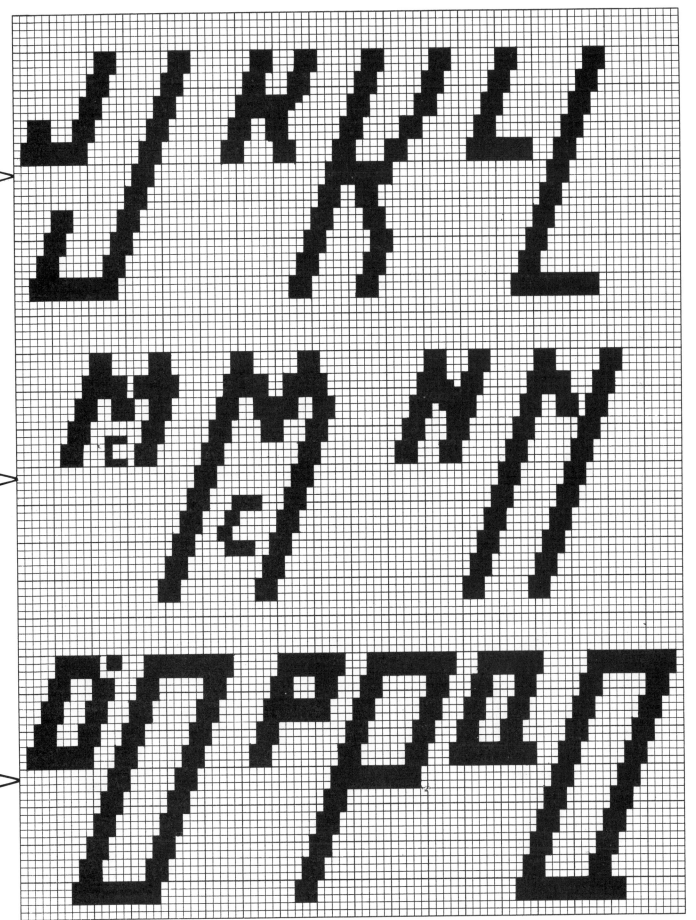

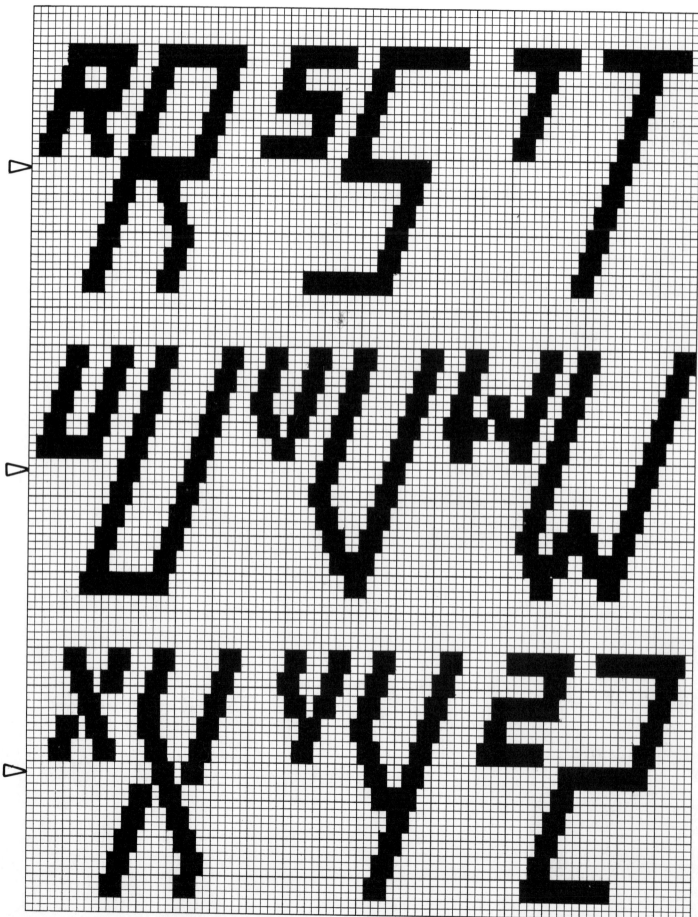

# Module 9  BARGELLO

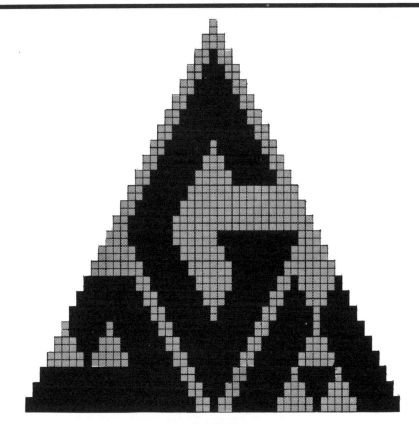

D.M.G.

C.P.R.

A particular feature of this module is that it can be worked up quickly in long, straight stitches.

The graph on the next page shows the basic units and the triangular building blocks in each unit. It will help you select and execute appropriate stitch patterns as well as aid you when altering any of the letter shapes to suit your particular needs.

Any stitch you can work over the smallest building block or triangle which covers 18 squares on the graph paper will work successfully for any letter in the module. You can use Vertical Gobelin over two-mesh, or use Brick stitch over four-mesh with a two-mesh step. A faster way to fill each triangle included in a letter is with a 2-4-6-4-2 mesh sequence of straight, vertical stitches. Tent, Cross, or two-mesh-high Oblong Cross will all work for these letters, but much more slowly.

Letter shapes may be nested or overlapped for more interesting compositions. In such cases, separate the letters with a line of backstitching, or by a single mesh or gate.

98

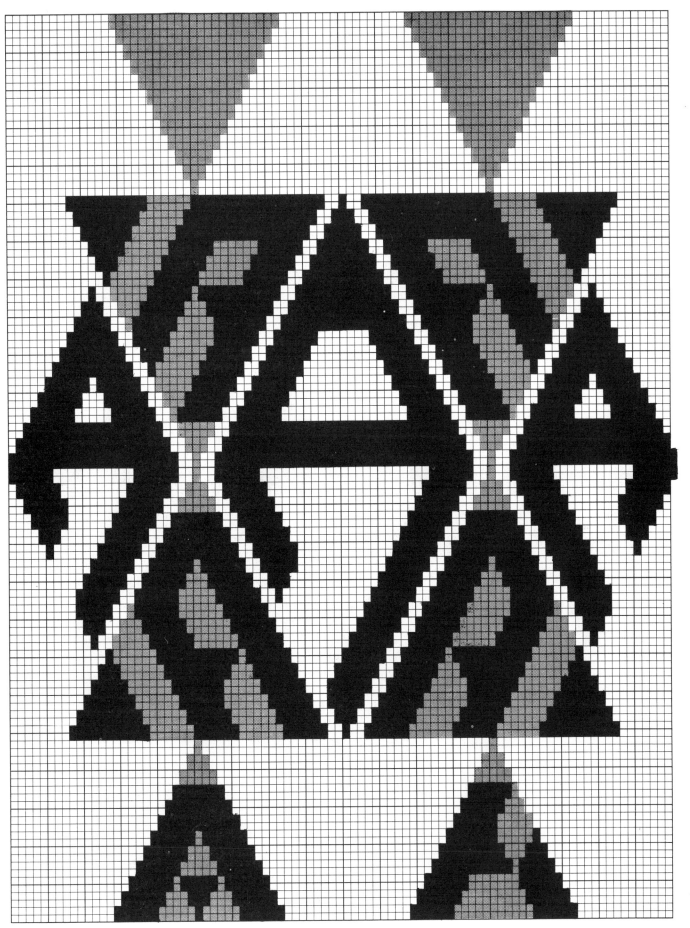

99

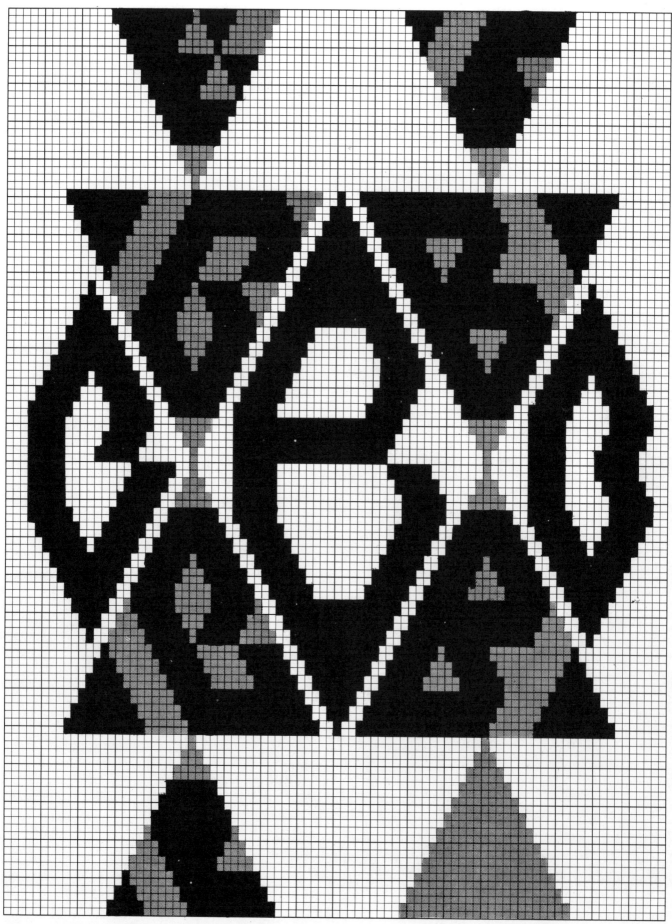

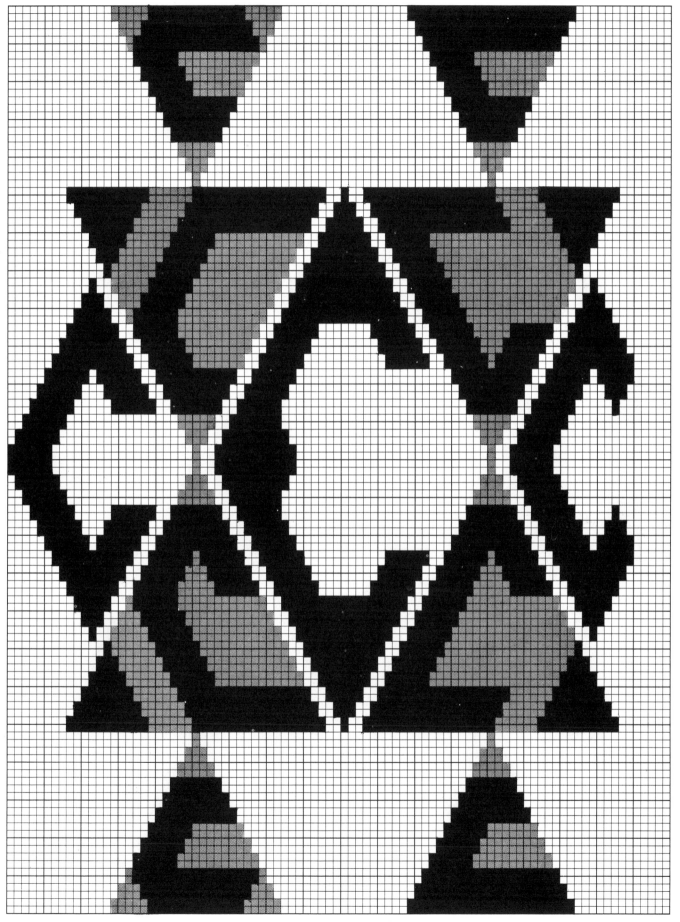

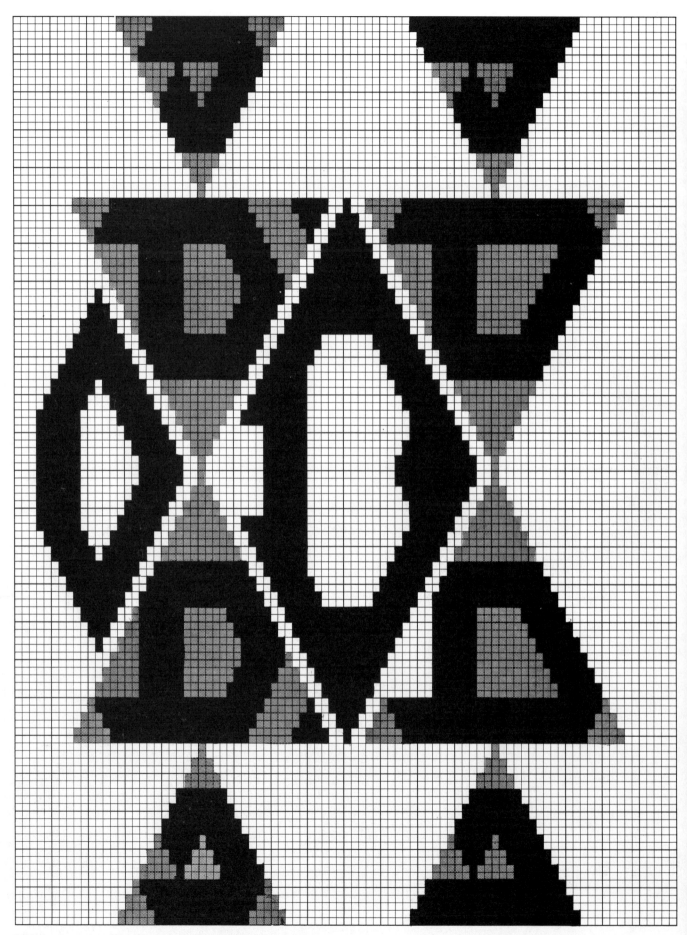

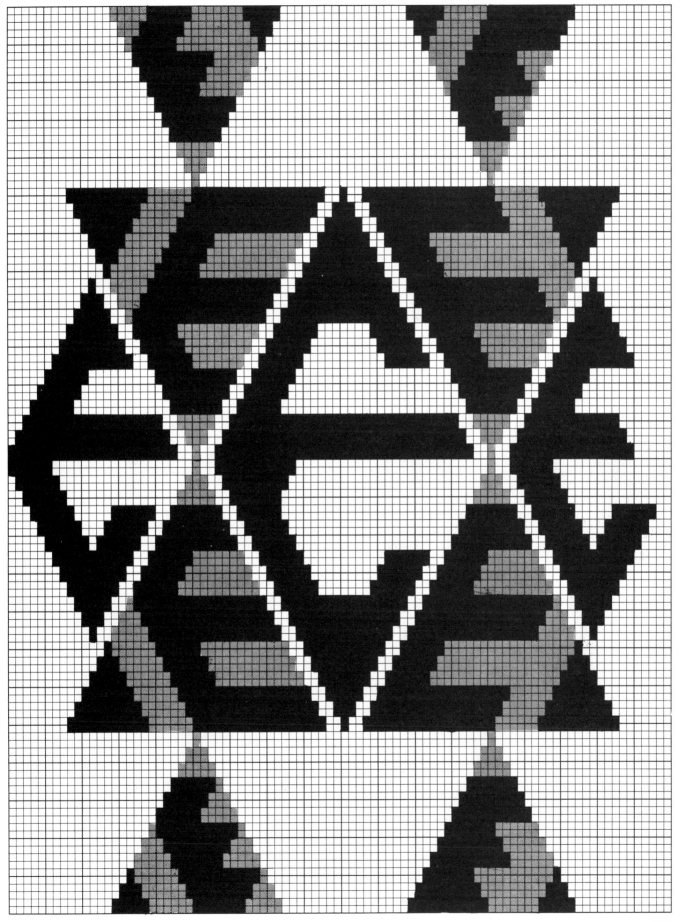

103

104

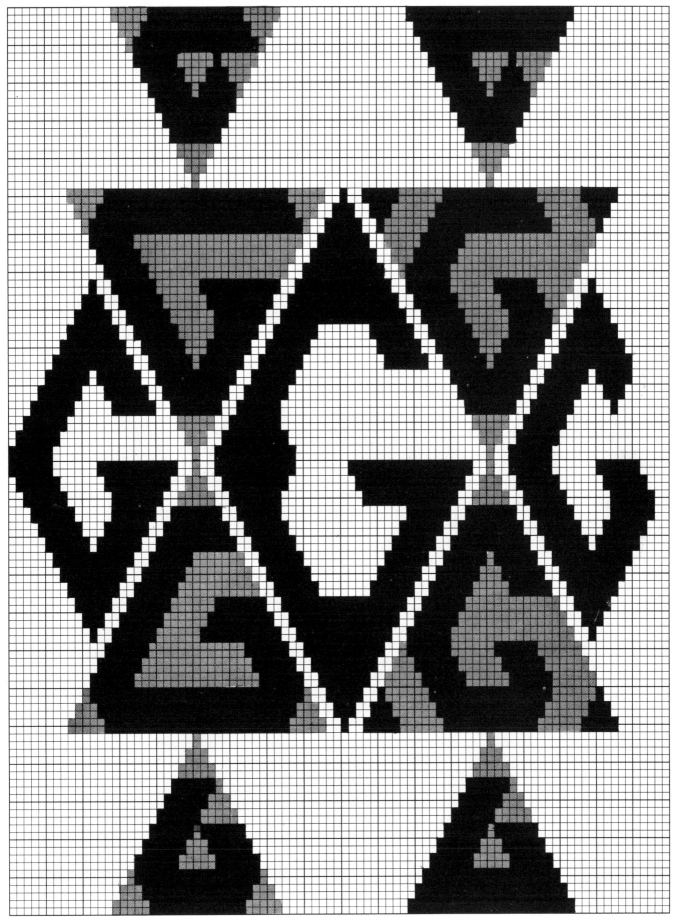

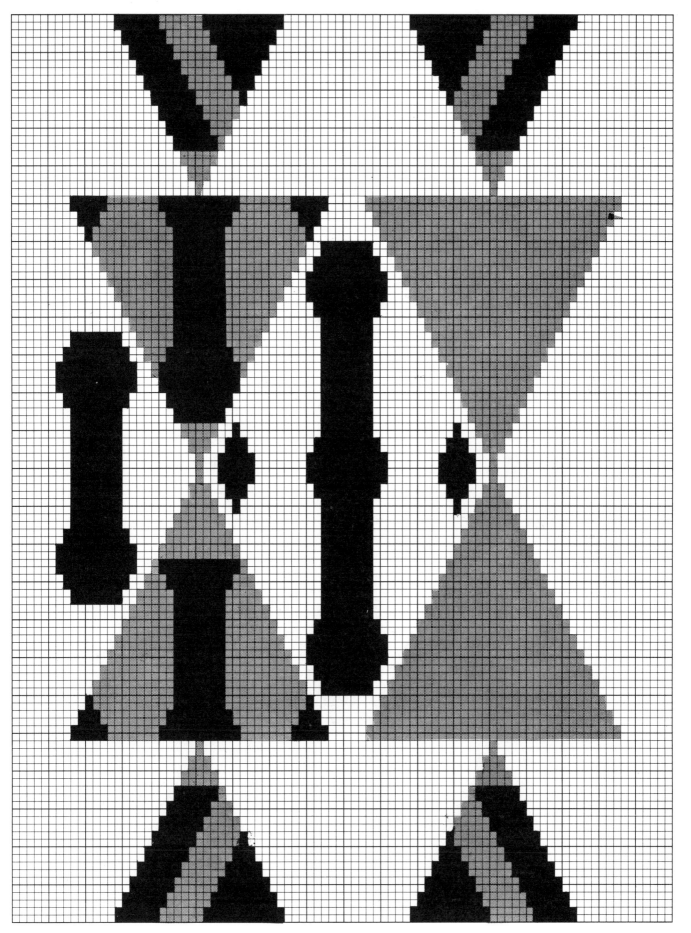

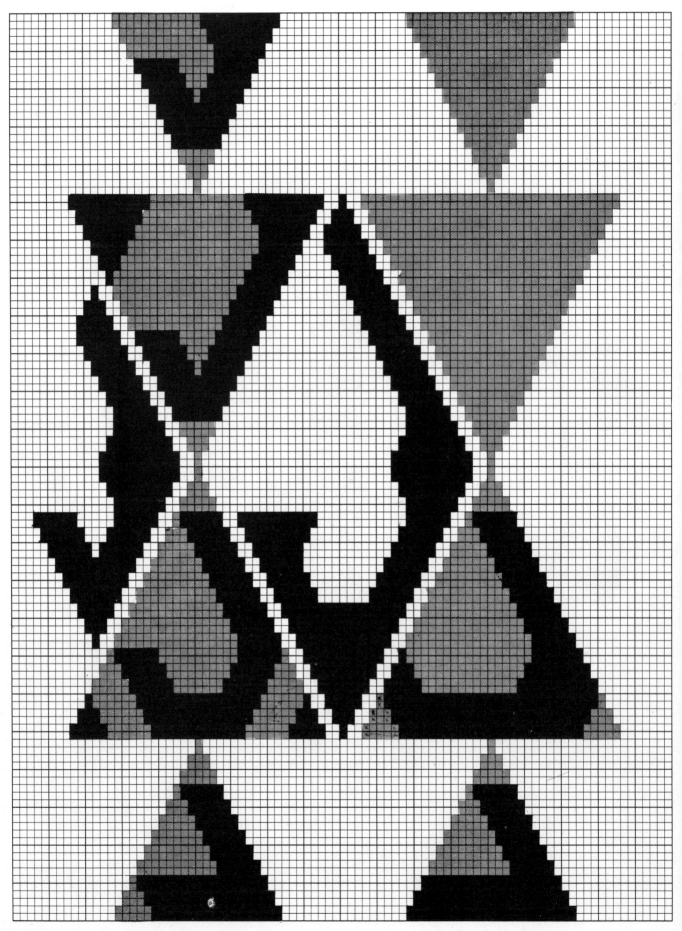

108

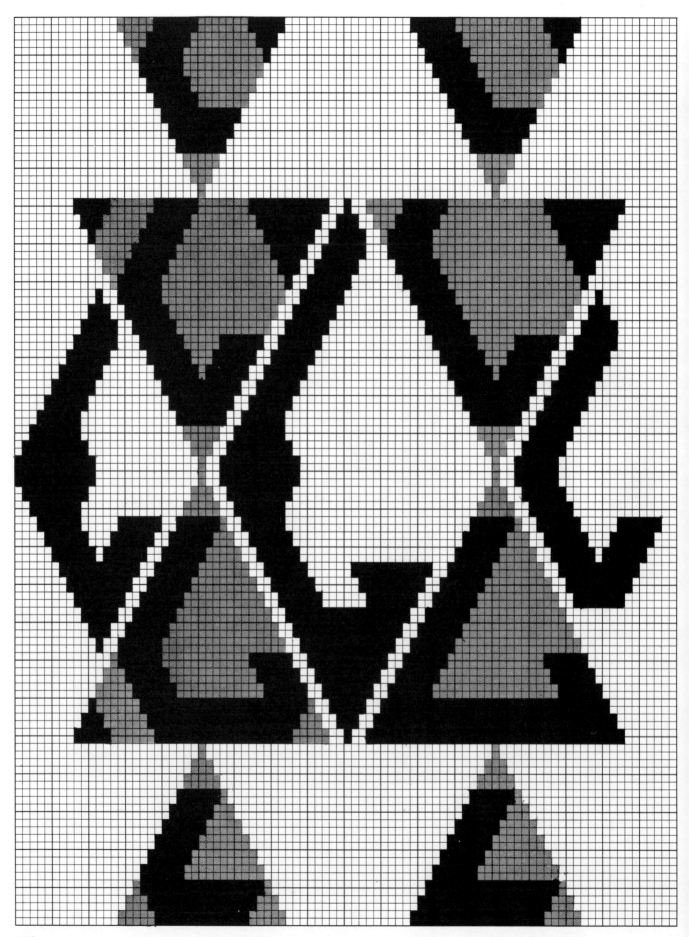

110

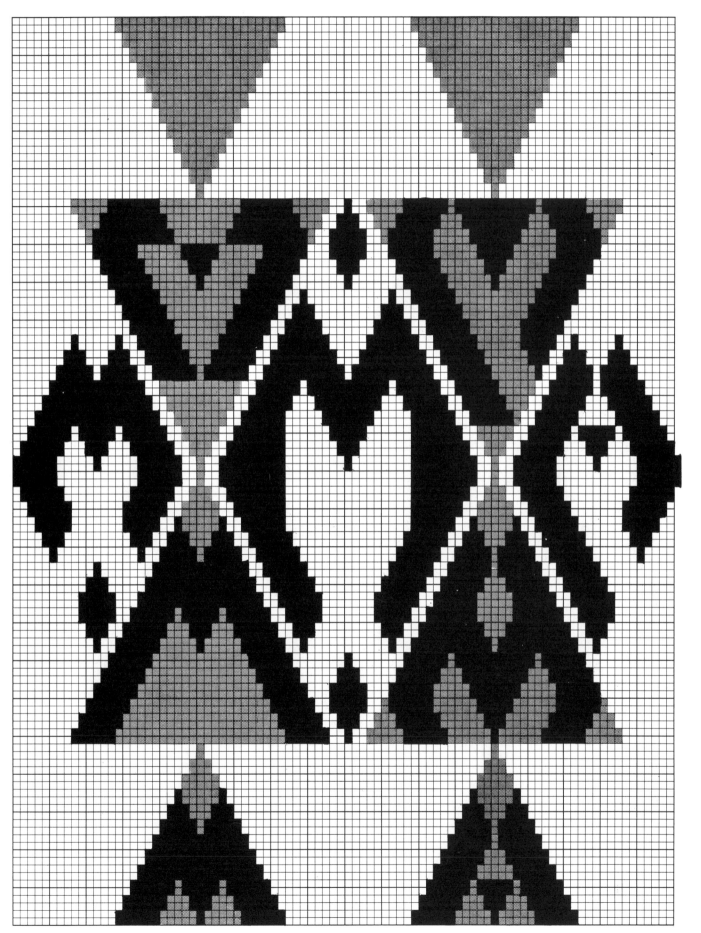

111

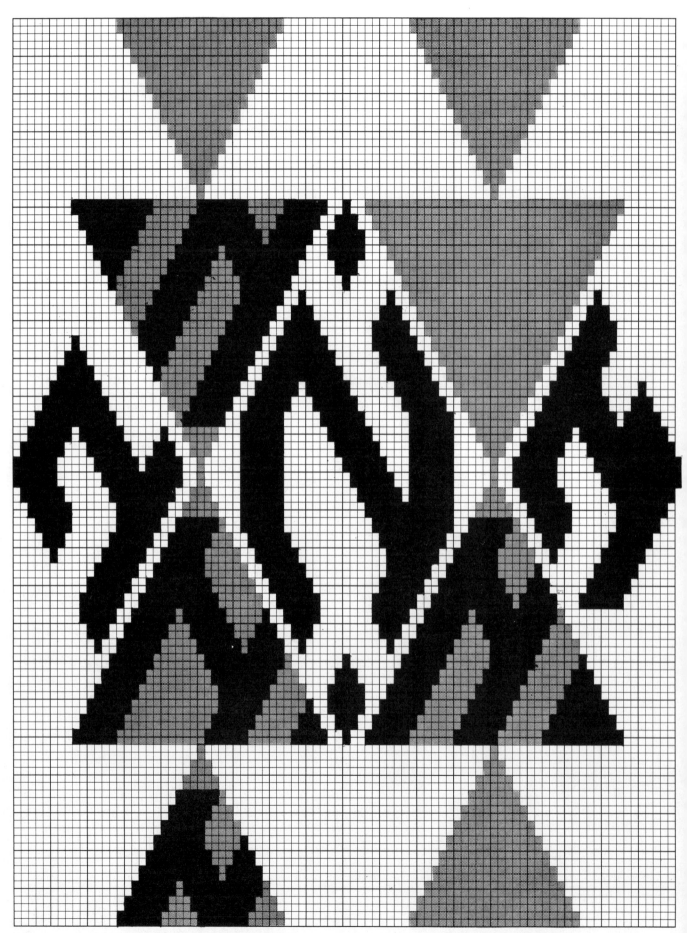

114

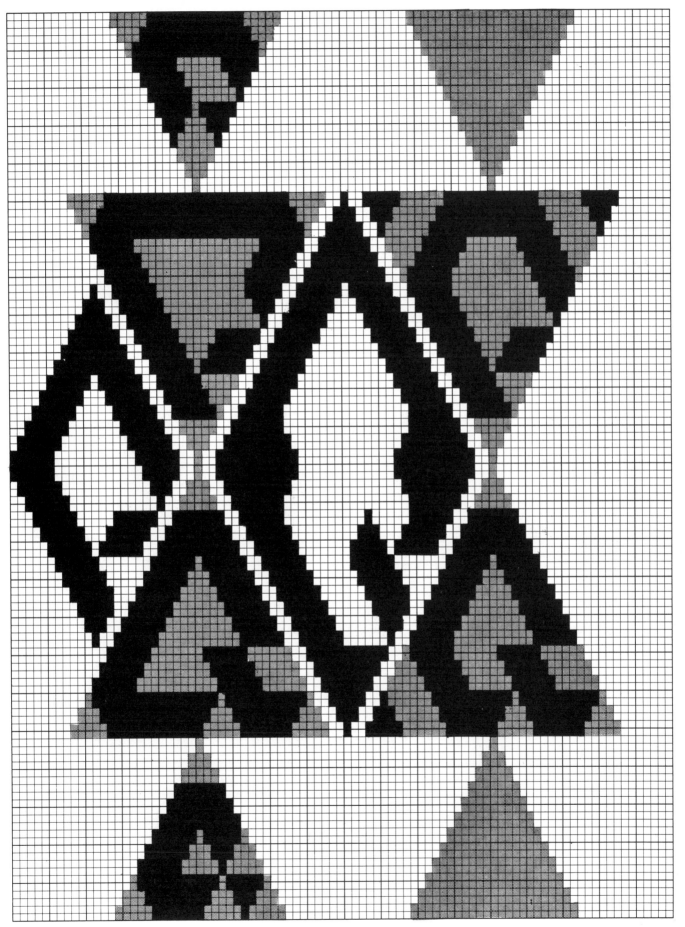

115

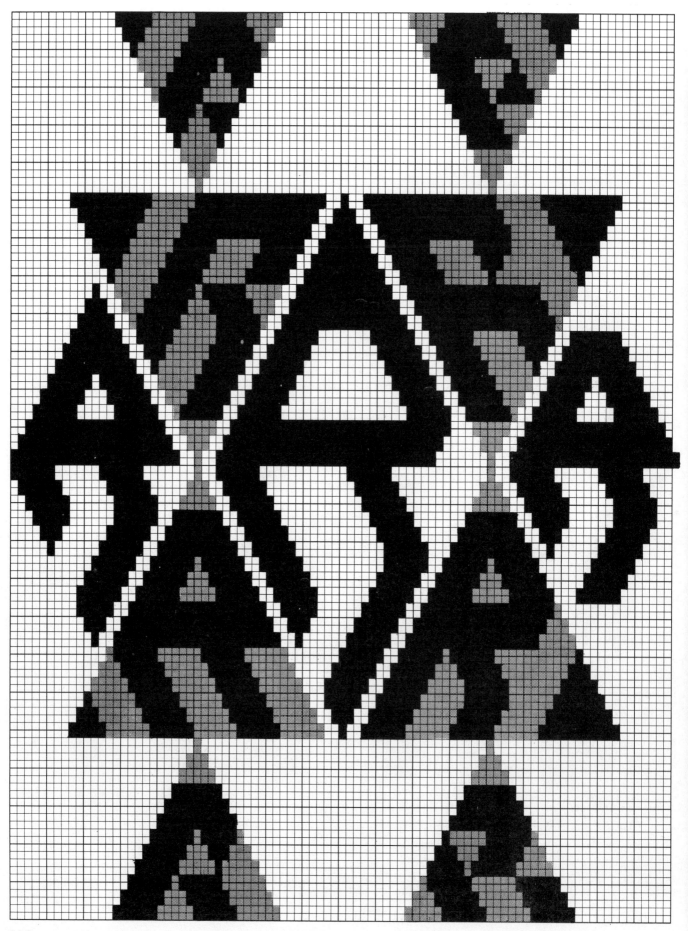

116

117

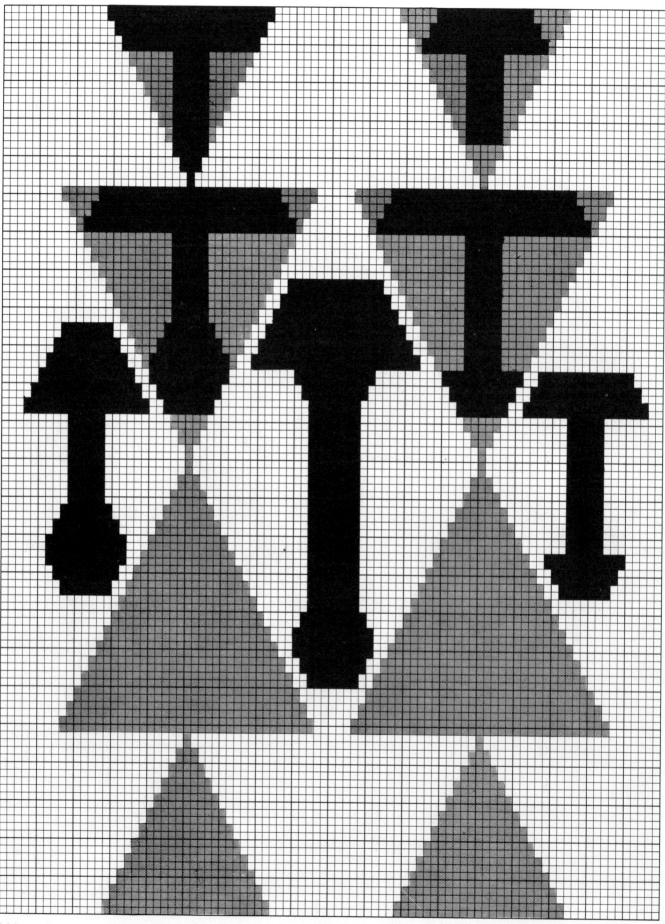

119

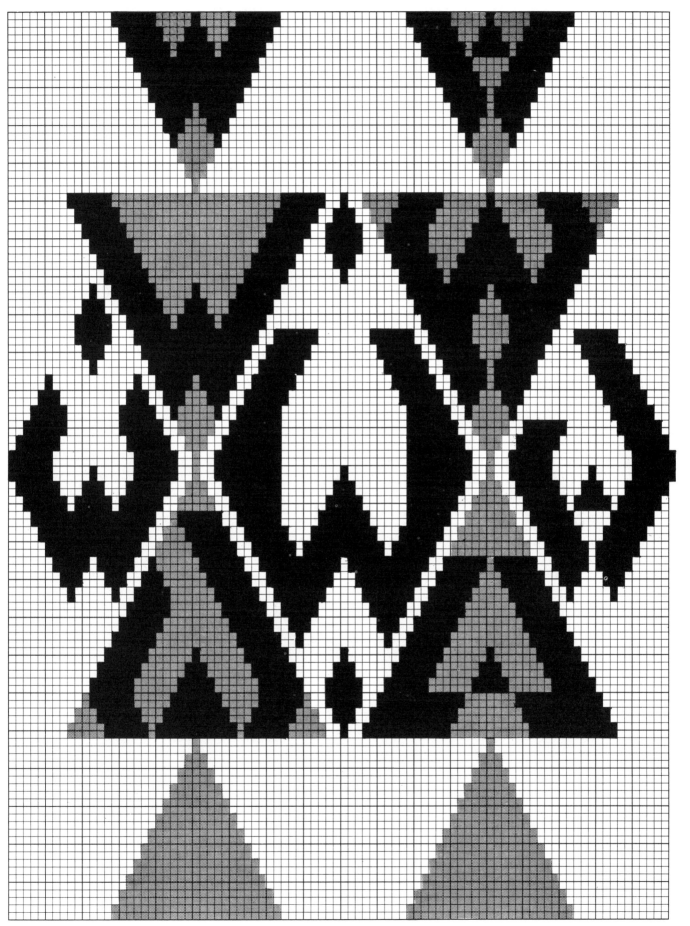

121

122

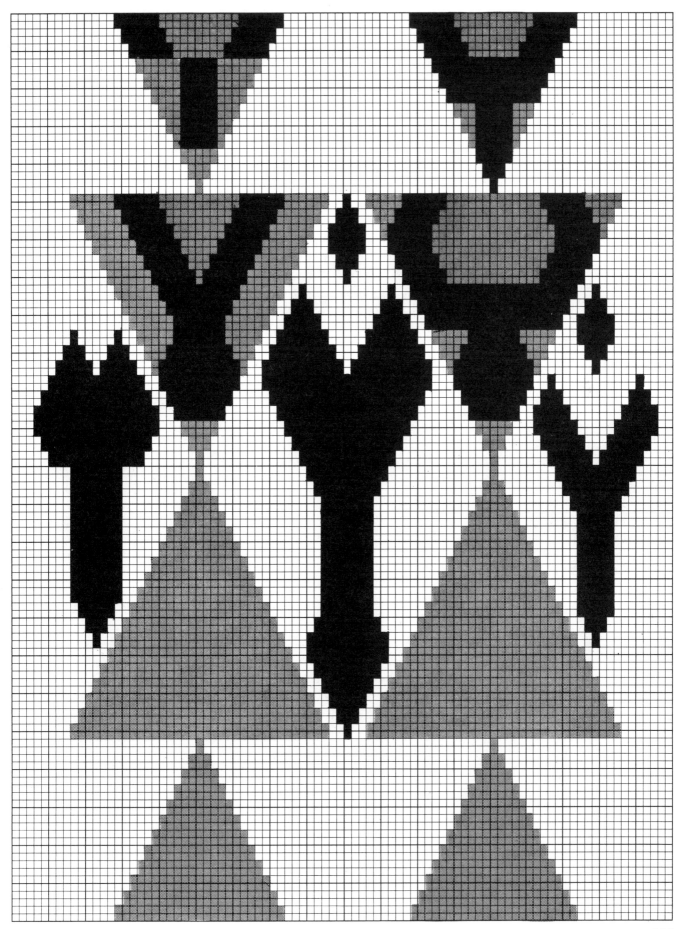

123

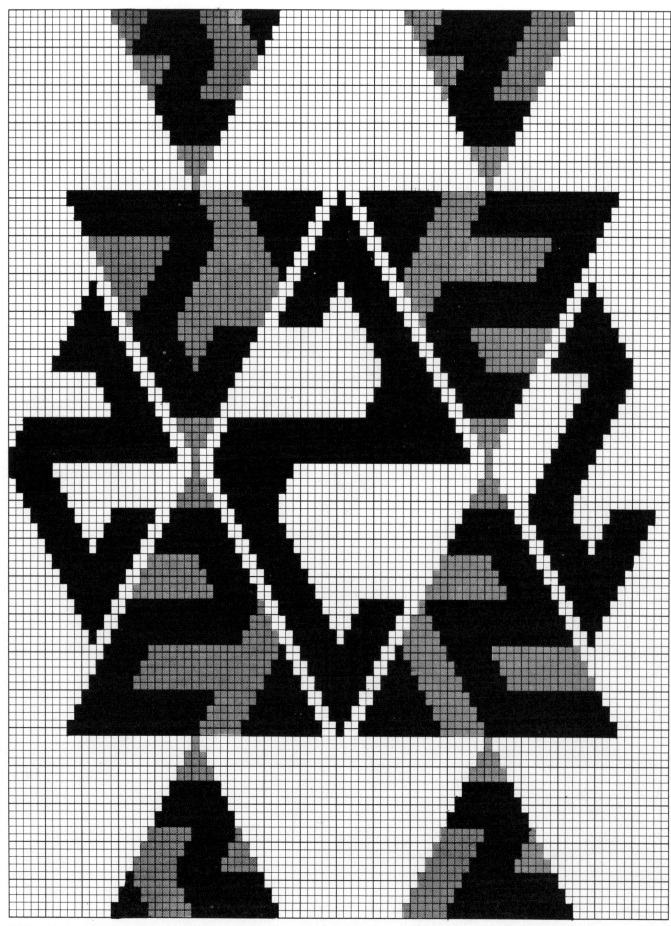

124

**D.W.B.**

Calligraphy is now in fashion. Therefore, these charted upper- and lowercase alphabets are included here.

Since these letters give the impression of being handwritten, monograms in this style should be done entirely in capital letters or entirely in lowercase letters. Proper names may be capitalized or not; both styles are accepted in contemporary graphics.

The letters are shown in solid black. The gray rectangles behind them may be considered the modular or design unit. They are also visual aids for the layout and counting stages of design and execution. Outlined areas are added flourishes a penman might give his work; you may or may not add them to your design. Such flourishes are constrained by space here, but you can—if you wish—sweep them across your canvas to help balance your composition or underline it with flair.

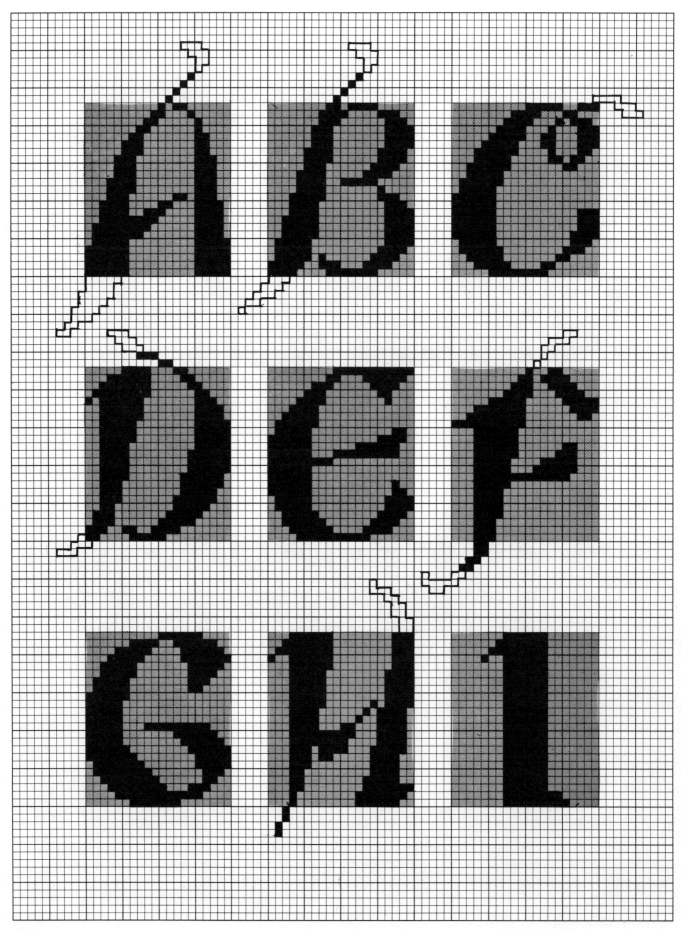

126

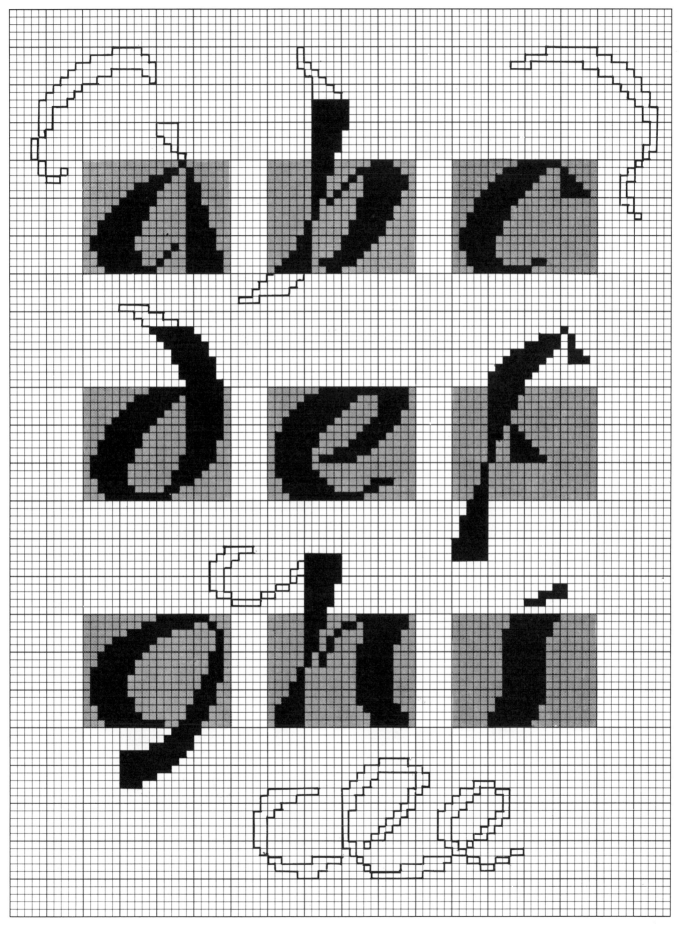

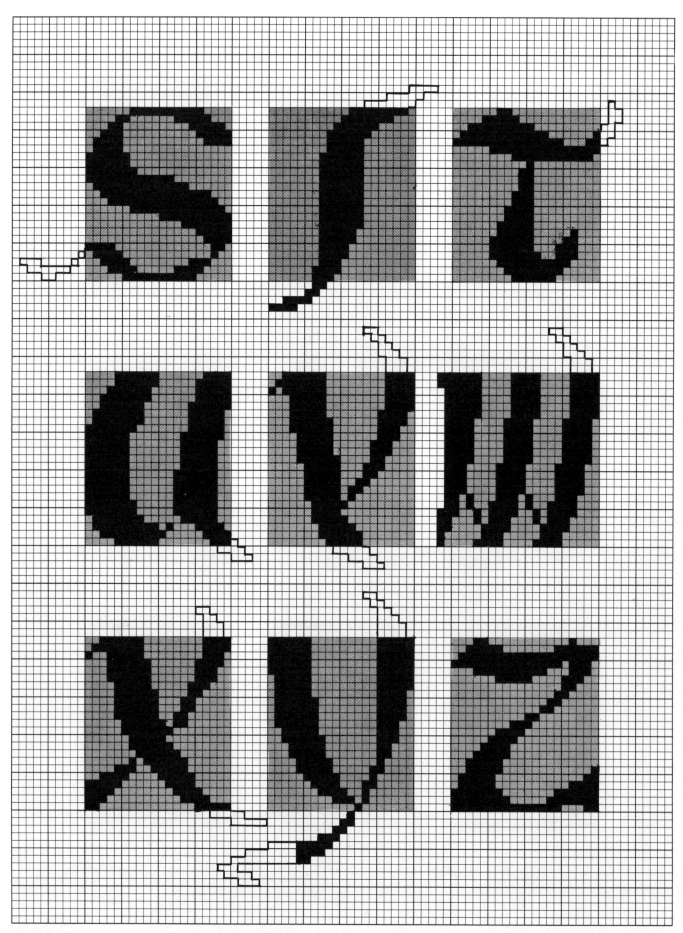

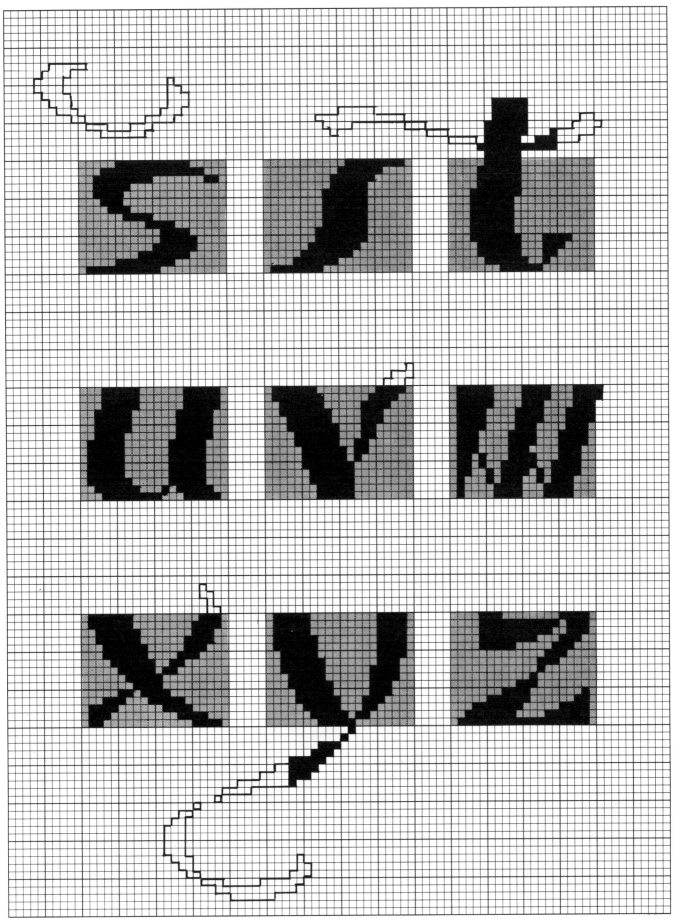

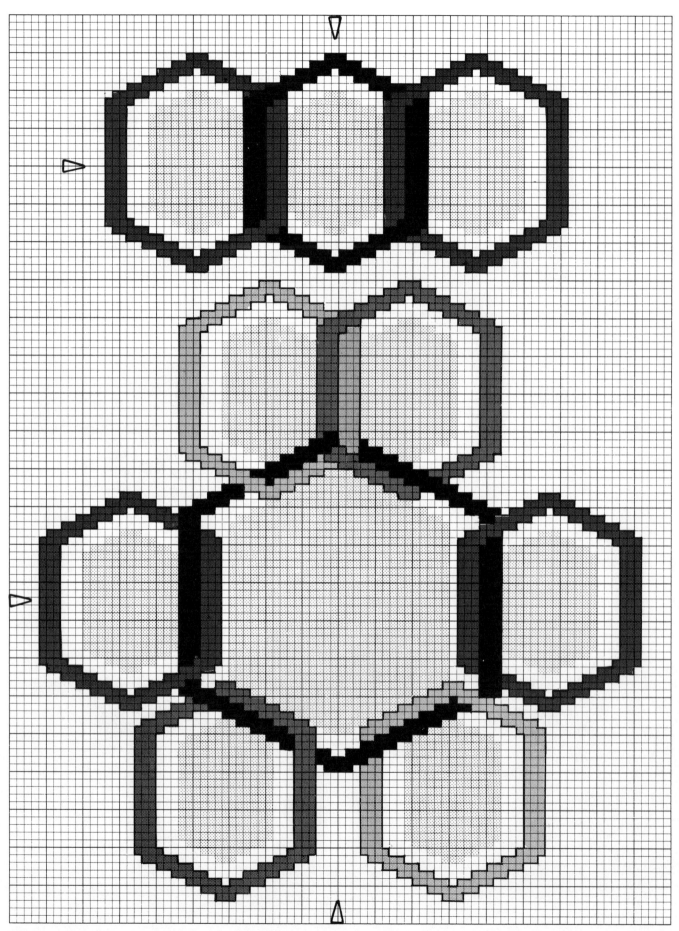

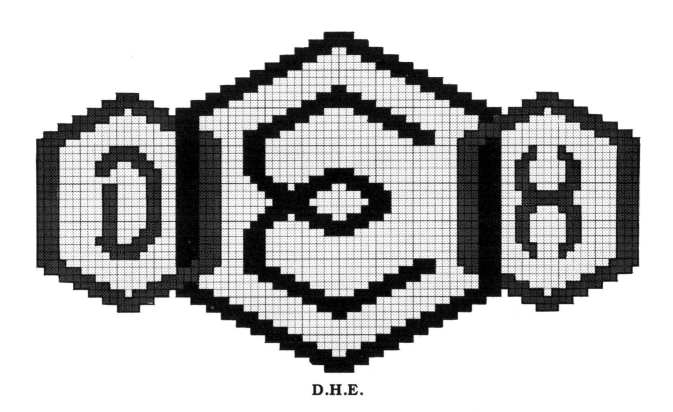

**D.H.E.**

The two alphabets in this module may be used without the interlocking framing. Try arrangements of the same size letters in horizontal, vertical, or diagonal lines. Try overlapping or intertwining the letters. Experiment with designs that use both sizes.

On the preceding page, frames are shown in a composite of interlocking positions. You may use any combination of two, three, or more links. Though not shown, the larger frame may also be connected into a two- or three-link chain similar

to the illustration that uses the small links.

Different shades of gray define the over-under sequence of the linkage, but there are several ways to get the same effect in your needlework even when you limit yourself to one color for all the frames in your design. Some methods are described in the introduction.

The gray areas behind each letter in the alphabets match those within the frames shown in linked positions; they will help you locate any letter within a link.

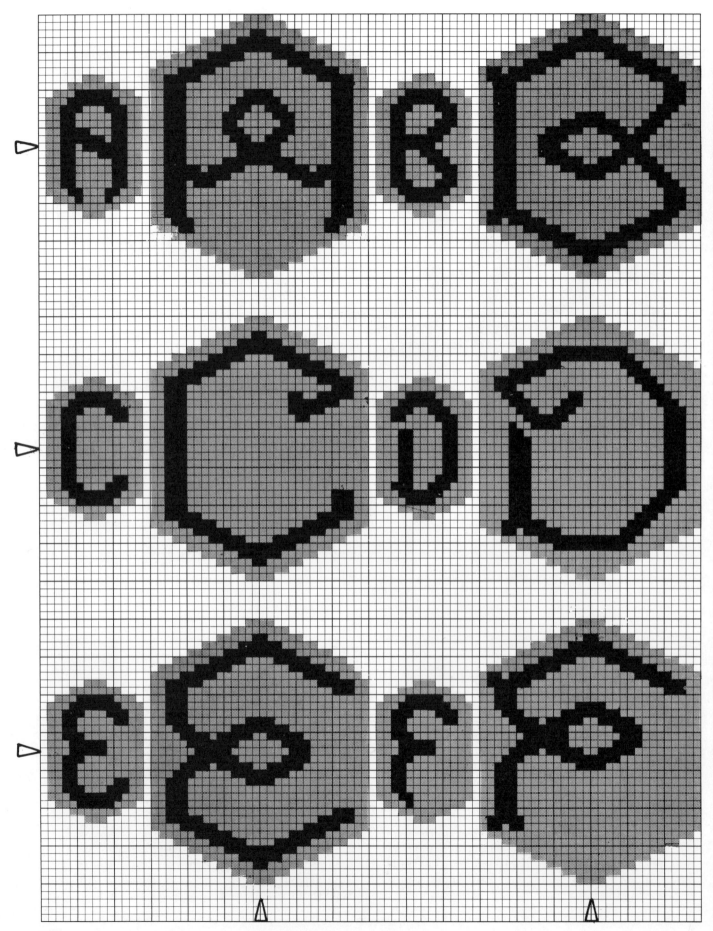

134

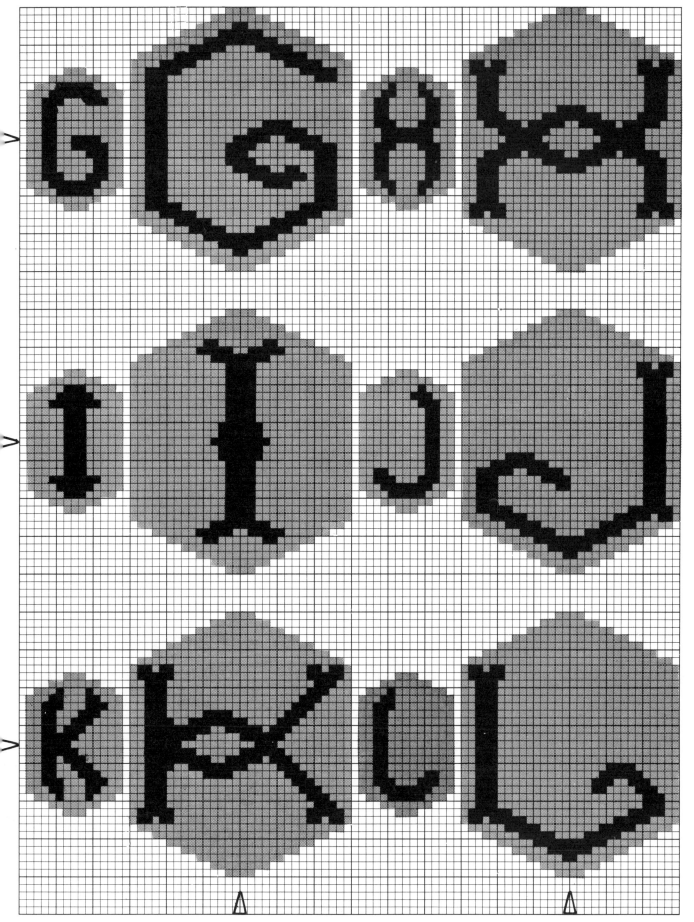

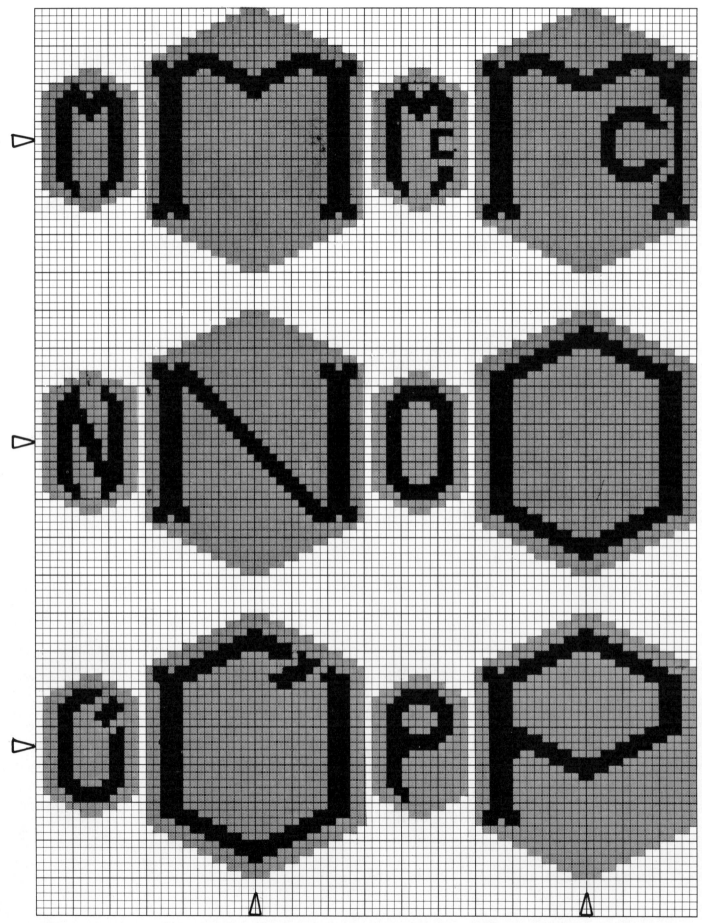

136

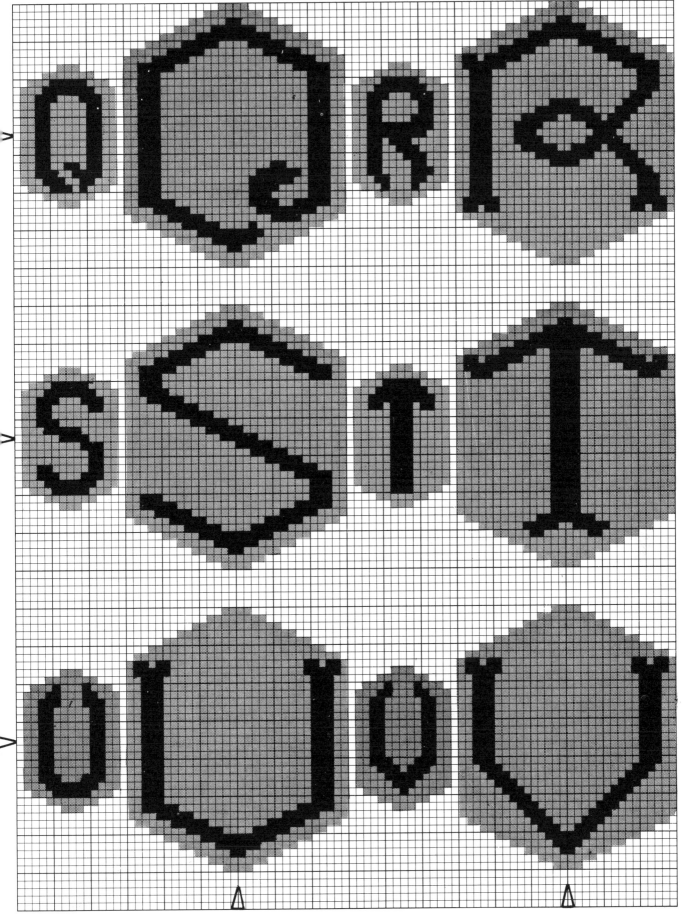

137

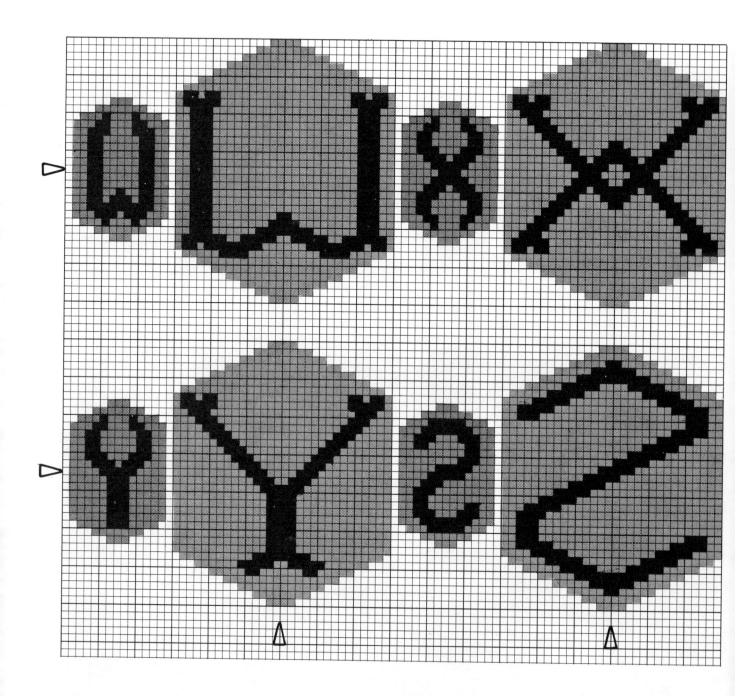

# Module 12   INTERMESH

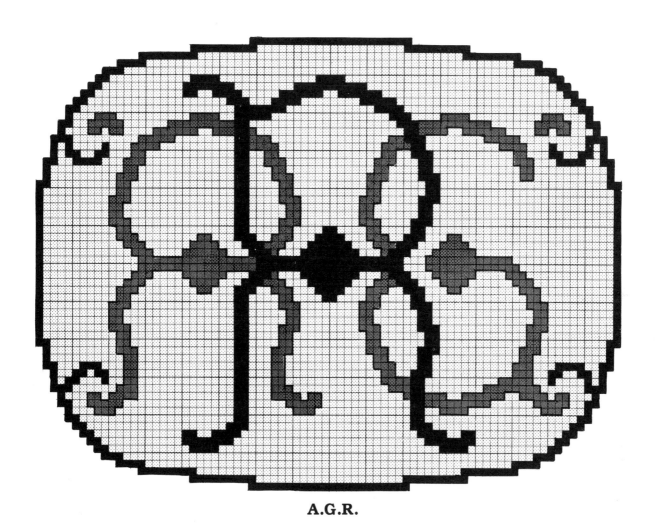

**A.G.R.**

If you can use three-letter monograms, you can take advantage of the unusual feature of this module, which is that any letter can intermesh with any other letter of another size.

If you need a graceful initial, select any letter, embellish it with tracery, leaves, or flowerets, or enclose it in the frame shown here. Two-letter designs can use letters of the same size, but they must be lined up independent of each other.

The example in the lower left-hand corner of the next page illustrates the figure-eight skeleton or basic shape of all the letters except *I* and *X*. (The letter *I* is included in this module because it is needed often and may be used between two other letters. The letter *X* is not adaptable to this module

and was excluded.) The other figures demonstrate that any two sizes can mesh together like gears: large and small, large and intermediate, and intermediate and small. Arrowheads mark the centerlines of the letters. The number of squares between vertical centerlines—as shown by the arrowheads in these examples—must be maintained for proper meshing of letters.

Black and gray letters are used in the sample monogram and in the spacing examples so that intersecting points will show up clearly. If you render all three letters of a monogram in one color, separate the letters by using gates, lines of backstitching, or change of texture. These techniques are discussed in the introduction.

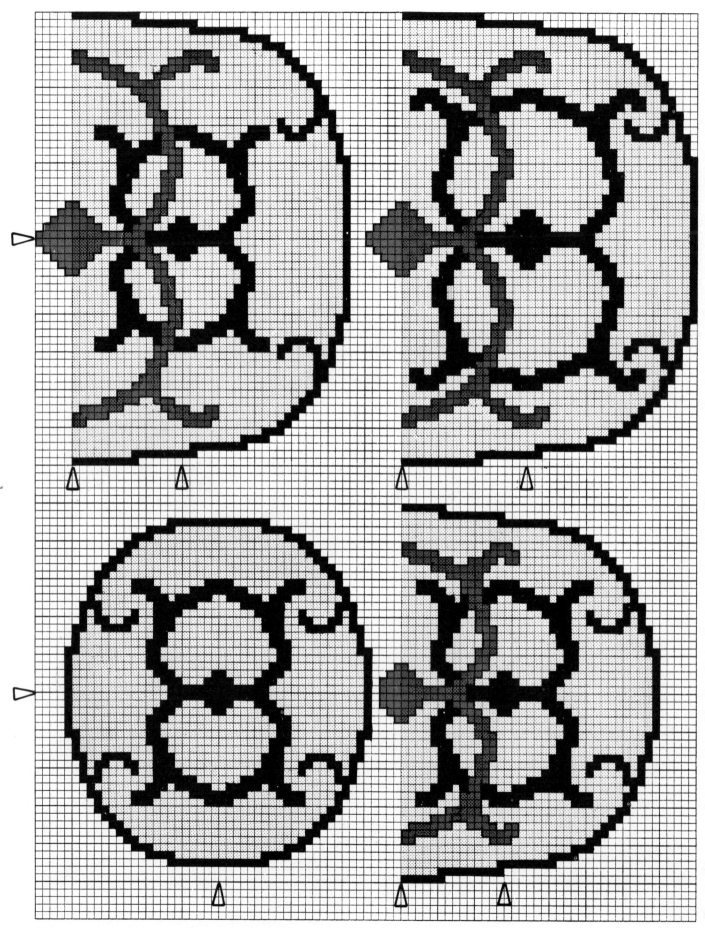

140

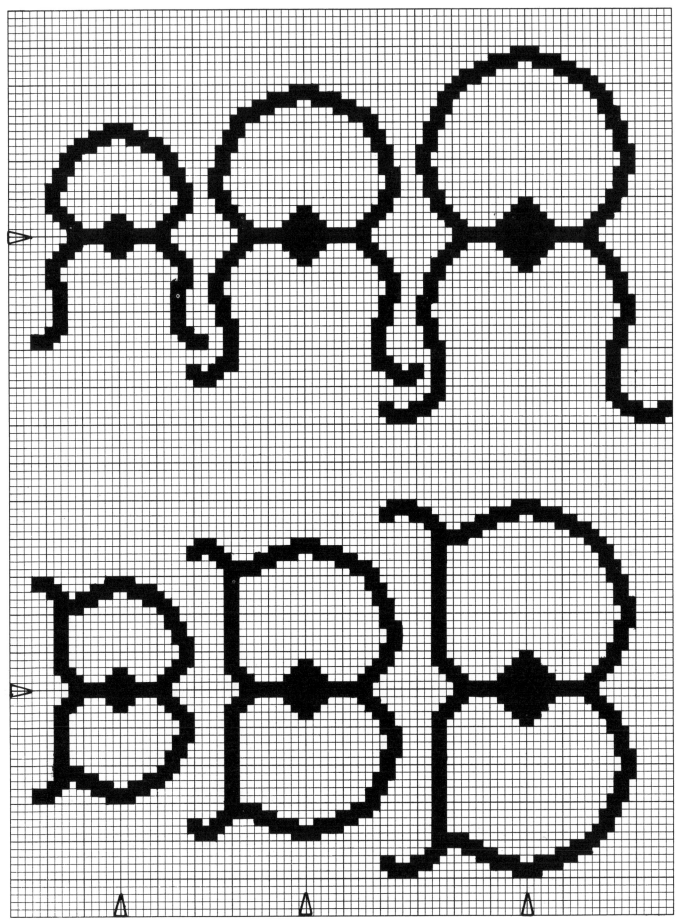

141

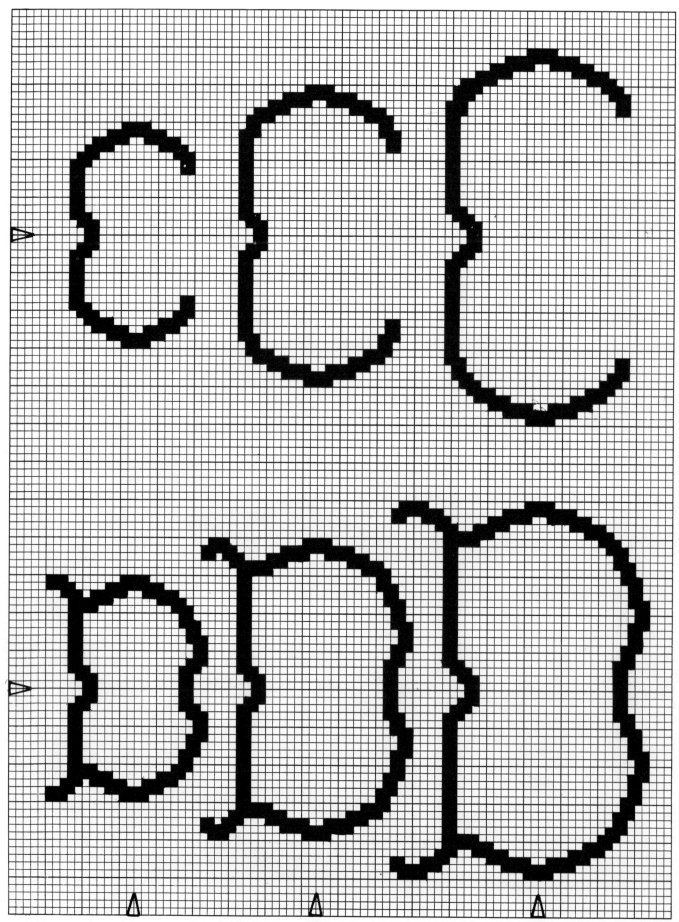

142

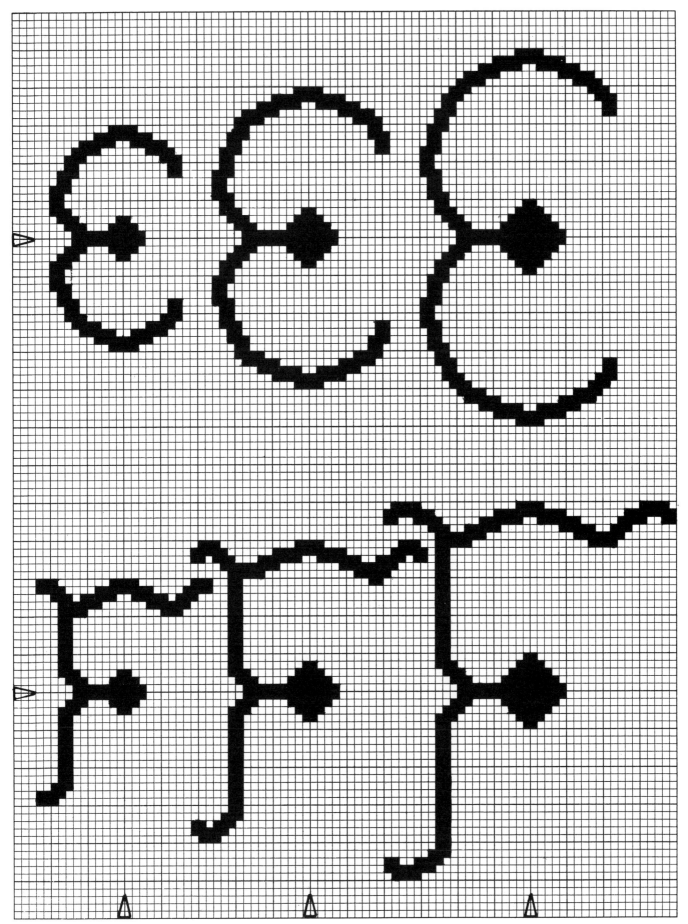

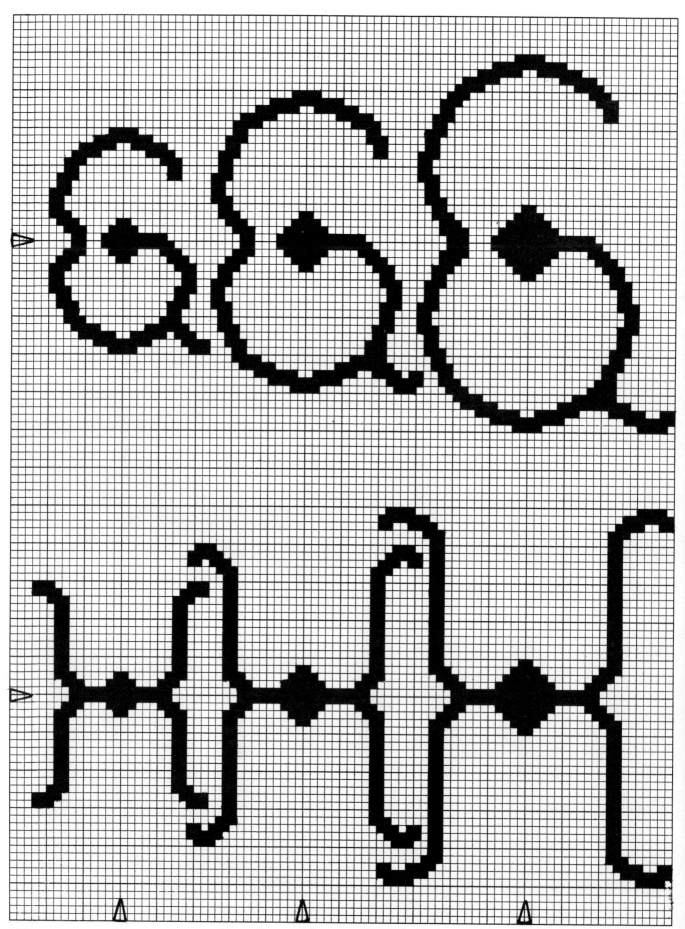

144

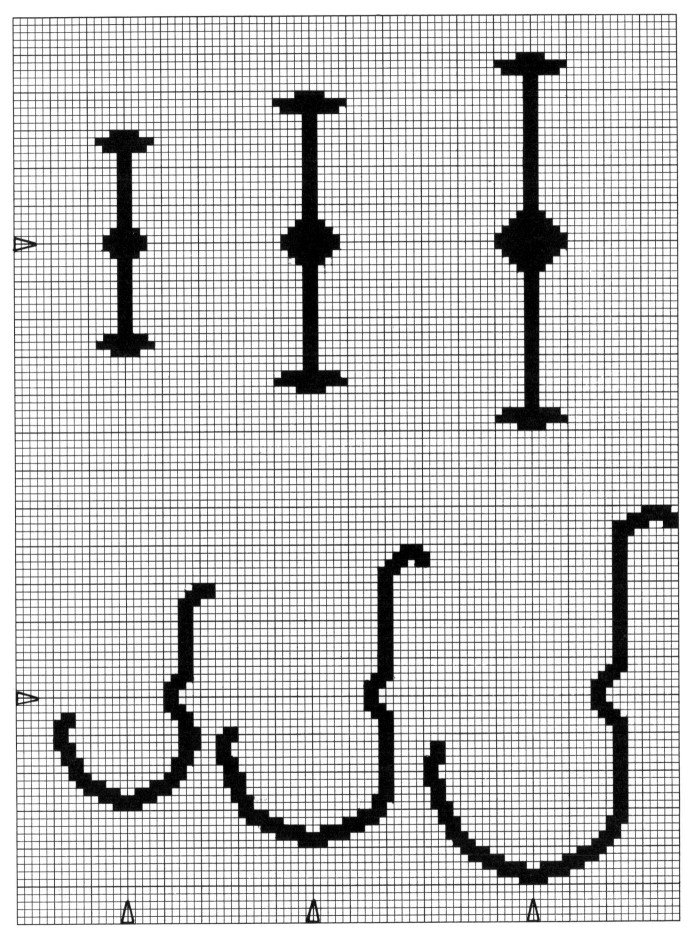

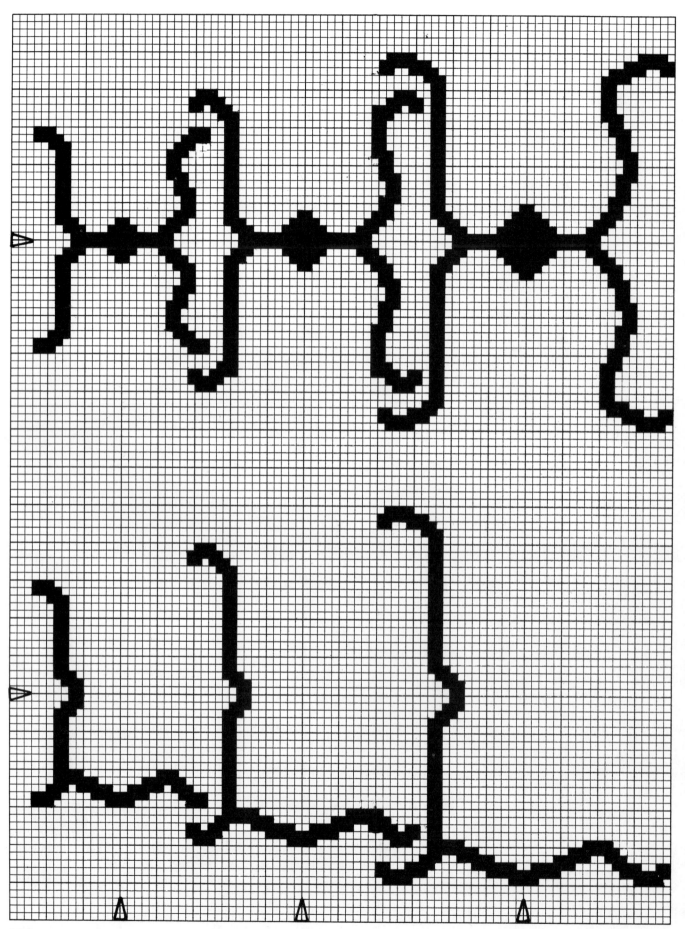

146

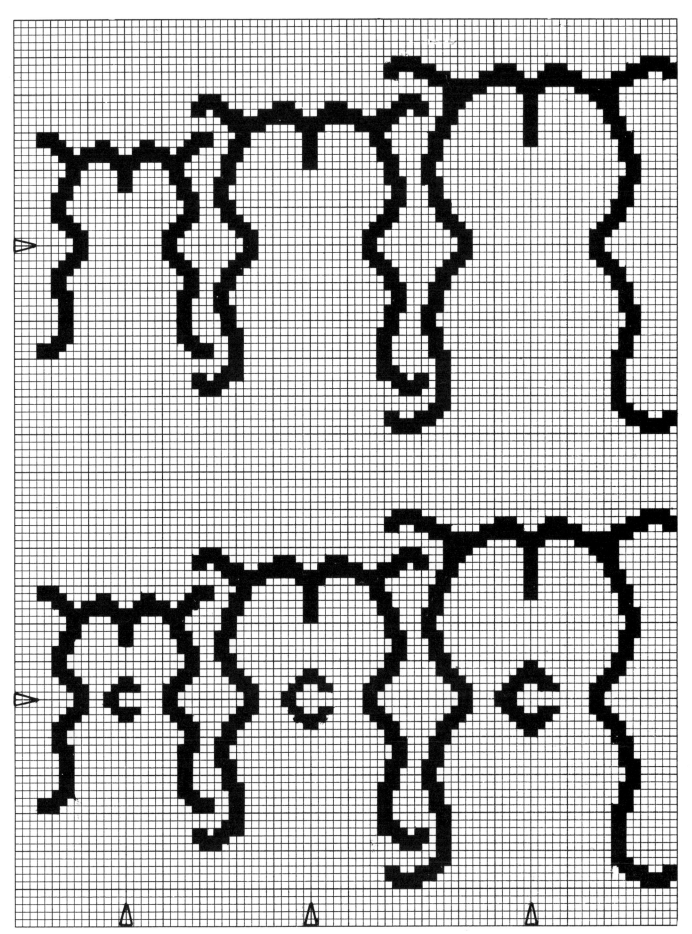

147

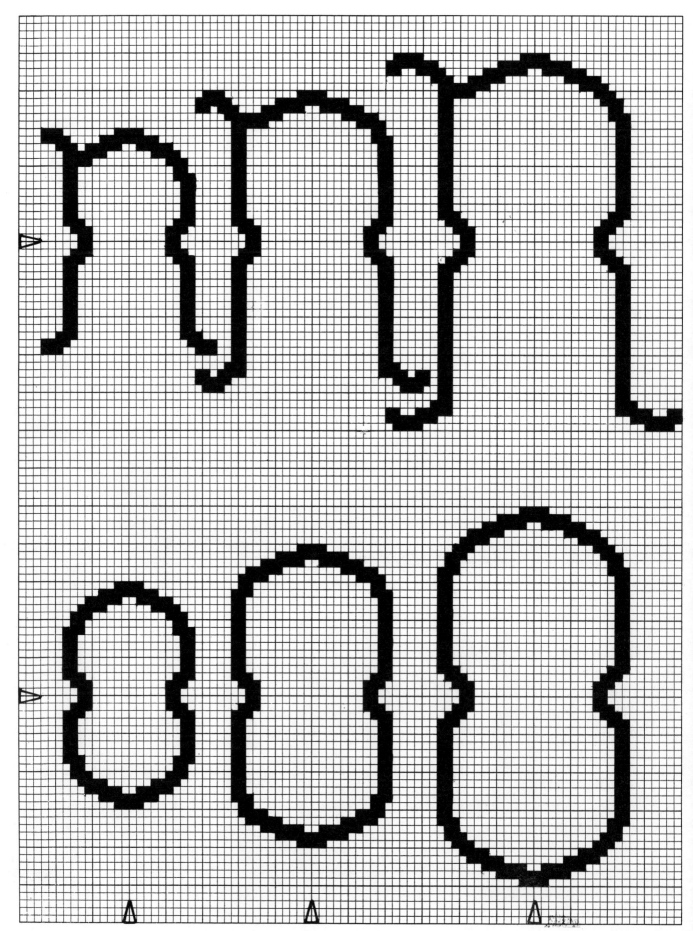

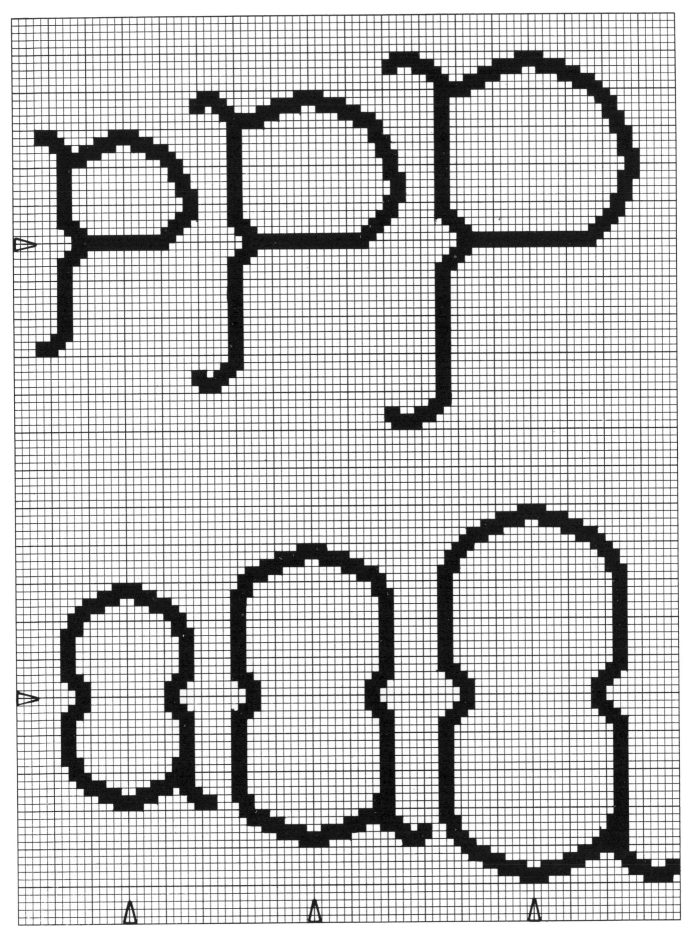

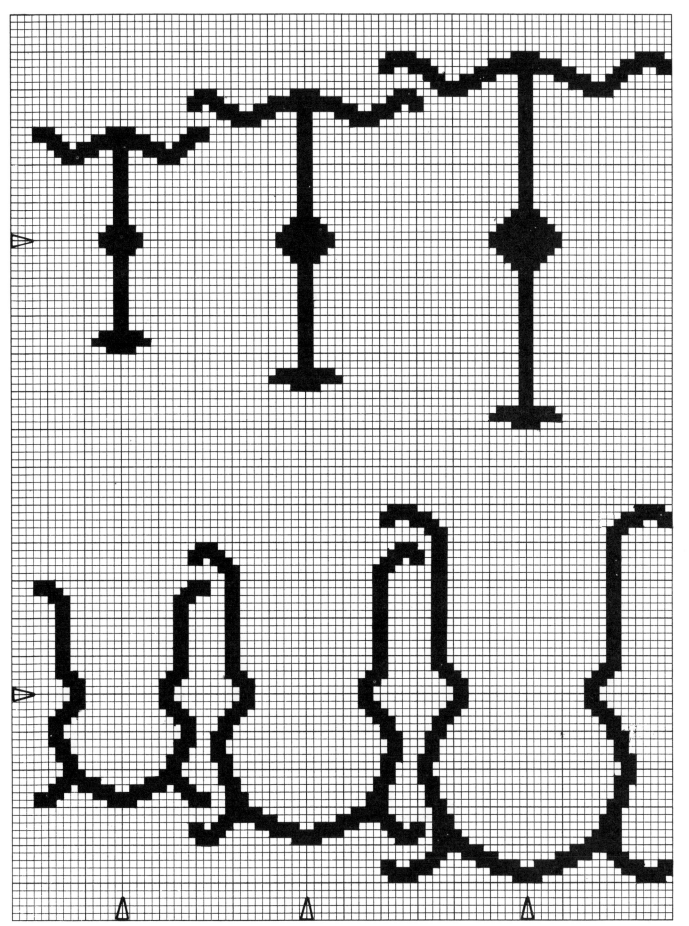

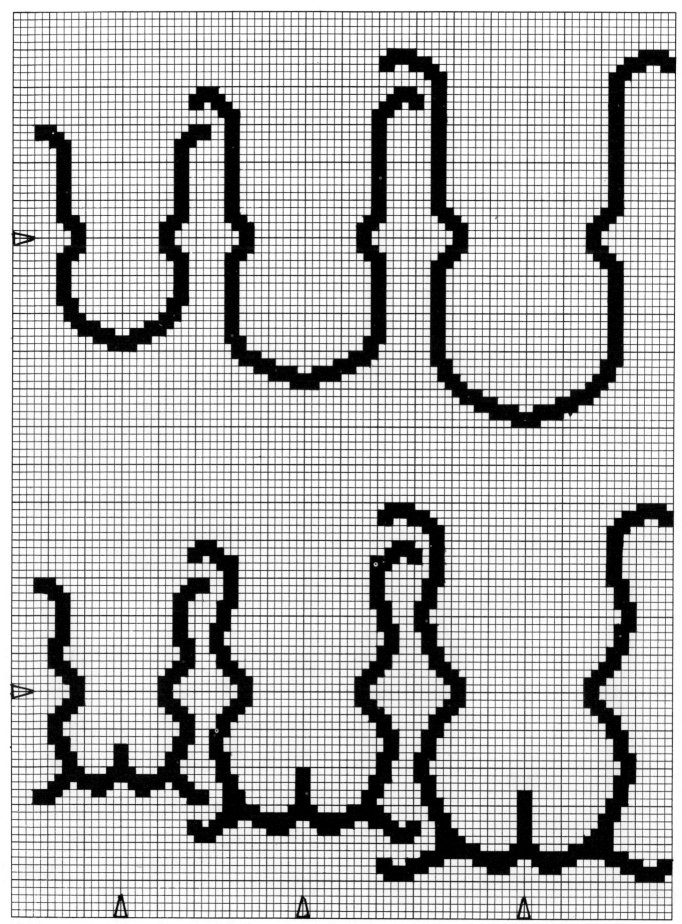

152

153

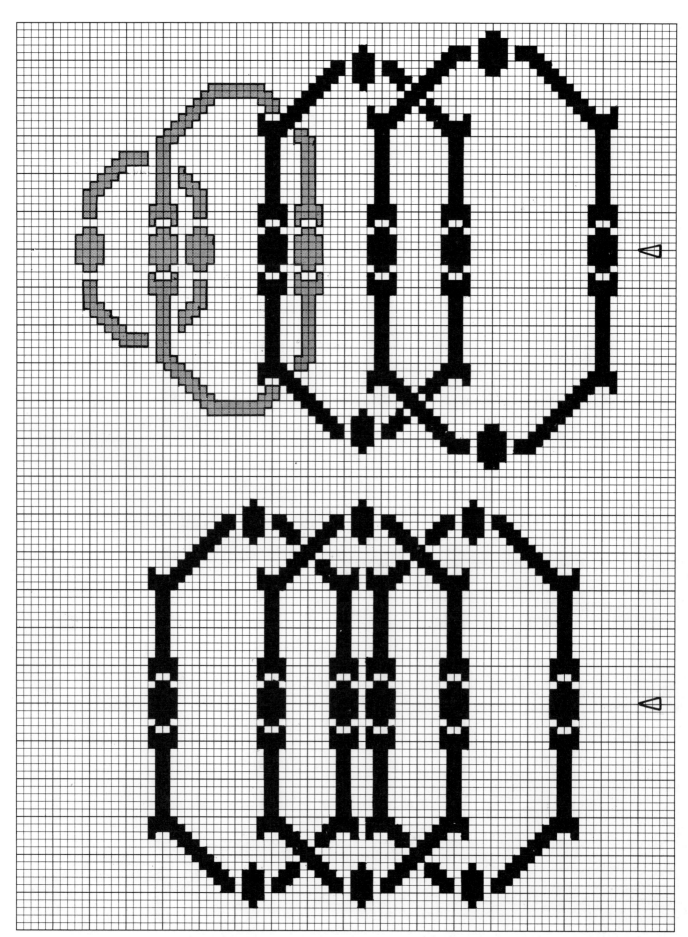

154

**A.M.D.**

The graceful letters of this module are unique because they can interlace with any other letter of the same size or with any letter of the other three sizes.

The A.M.D. monogram combines the smallest and largest sizes charted. All four sizes—small, medium, queen, and king—of the letter *O* are shown in interlaced position at the top of the preceding page. The series at the bottom of the page shows the interlacing of the queen size only. These letters *O* or ovals, plus a string of beadlike motifs such as those in the letter *A*, are the basic shapes of all the letters of the alphabet except *I*. To interlace any selection of letters, line up or duplicate the beads in intervals that make a pleasing arrangement.

Small and medium-size letters are shown in gray and are outlined. Queen and king sizes are in black. Letters are shown separated by gates at all intersections. You may vary the over-under sequence, or you may eliminate the gates entirely. Refer to the introduction for other ways to delineate two planes. Note, however, that the separations or gates next to the beads on the horizontal and vertical centerlines should be retained as part of the letter design.

Tent stitch, any vertical or horizontal straight stitch, or Cross stitch may be used. The last-named will show these letters to good advantage while giving excellent coverage and an interesting texture.

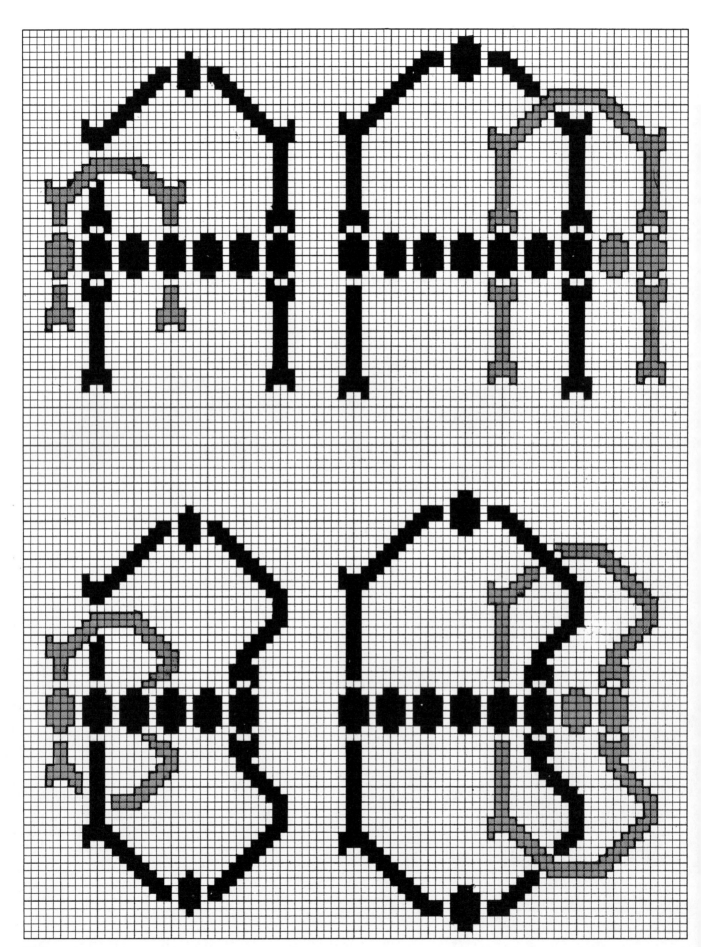

156

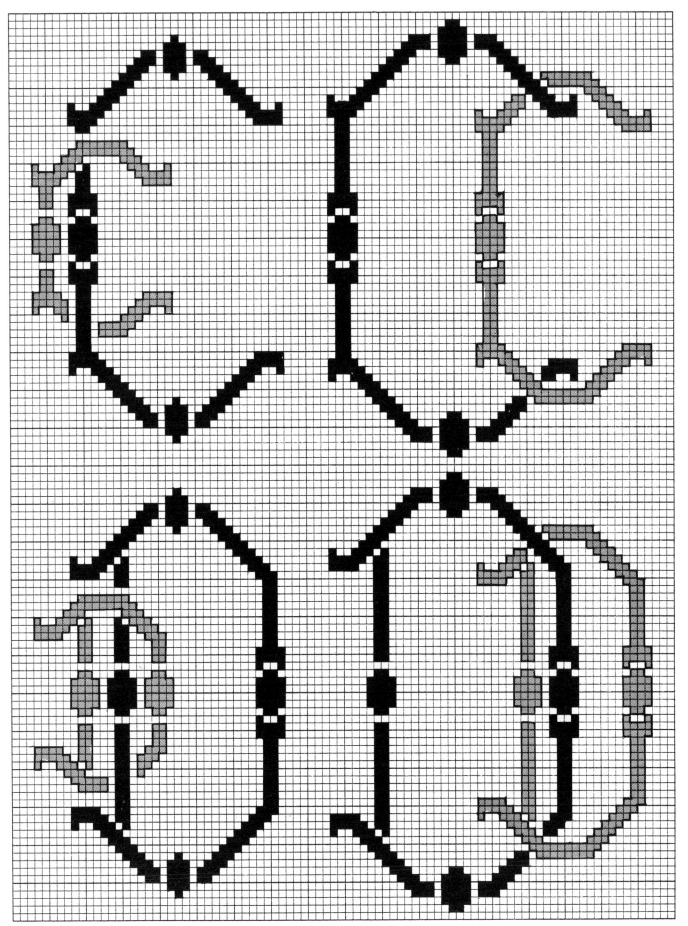

157

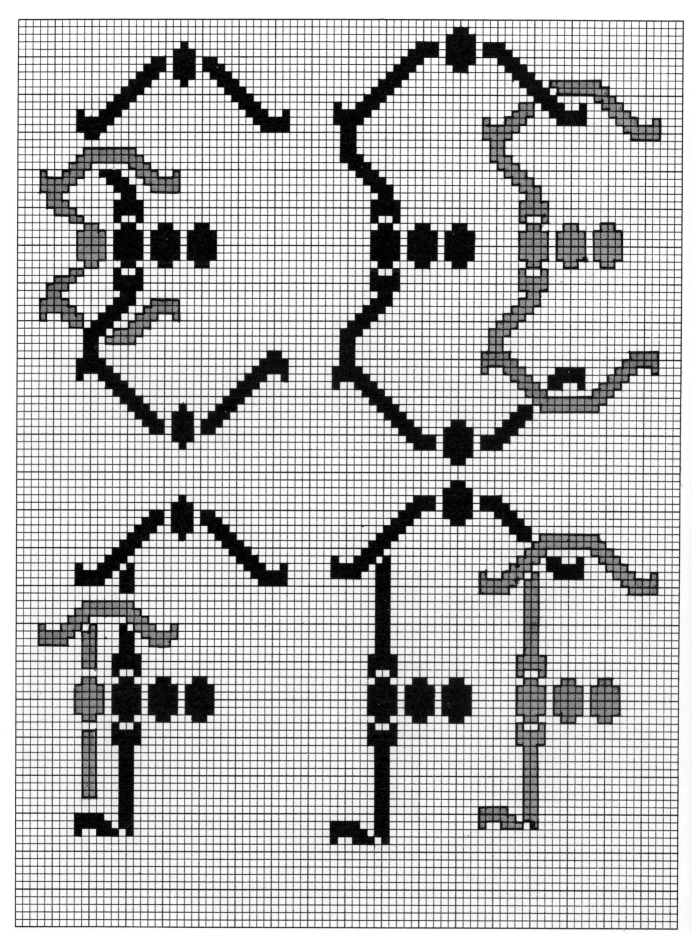

158

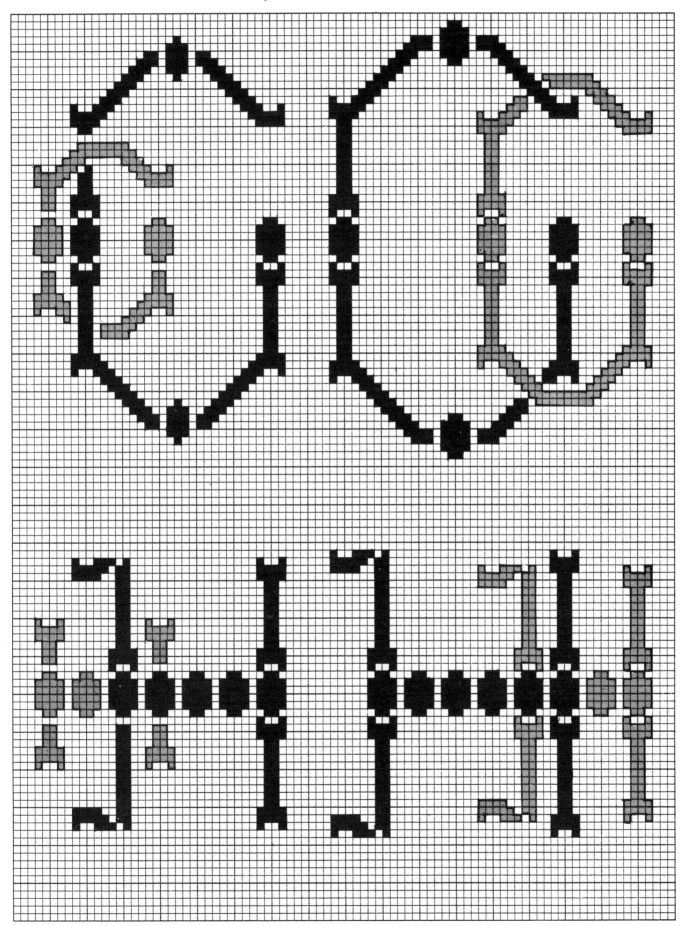

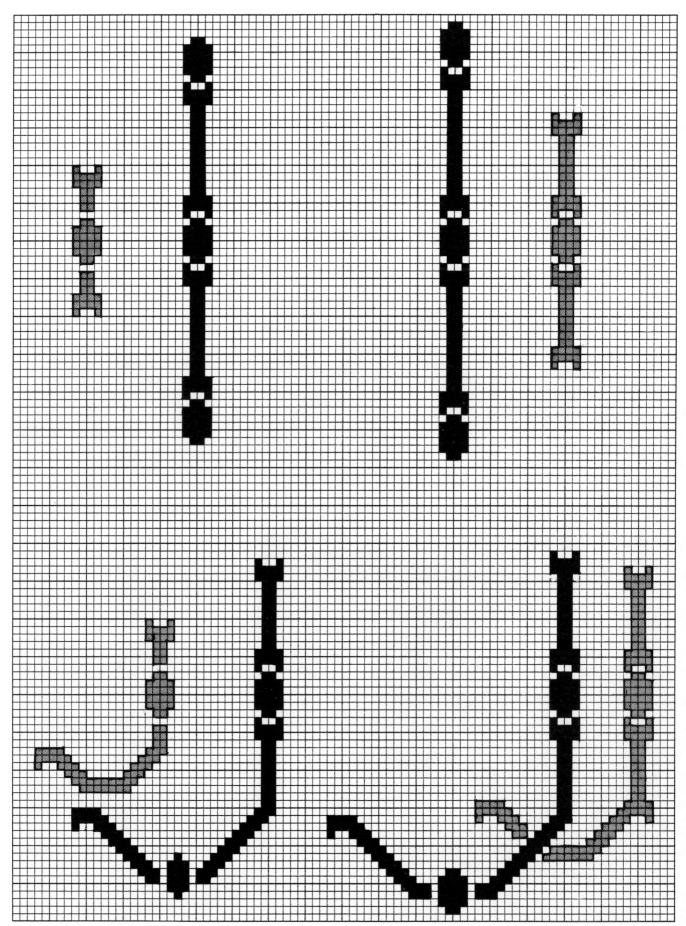

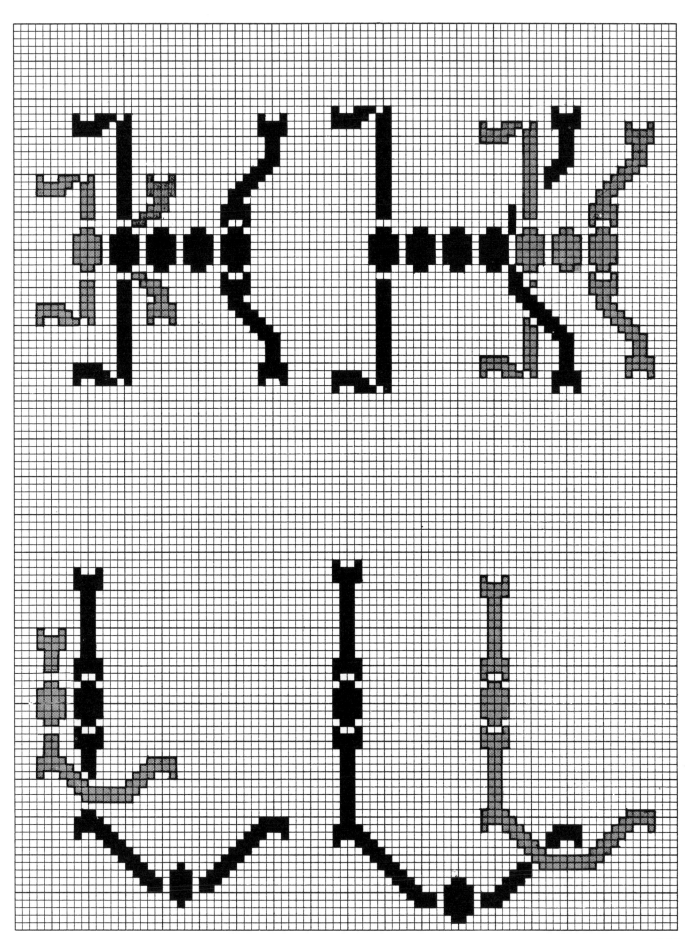

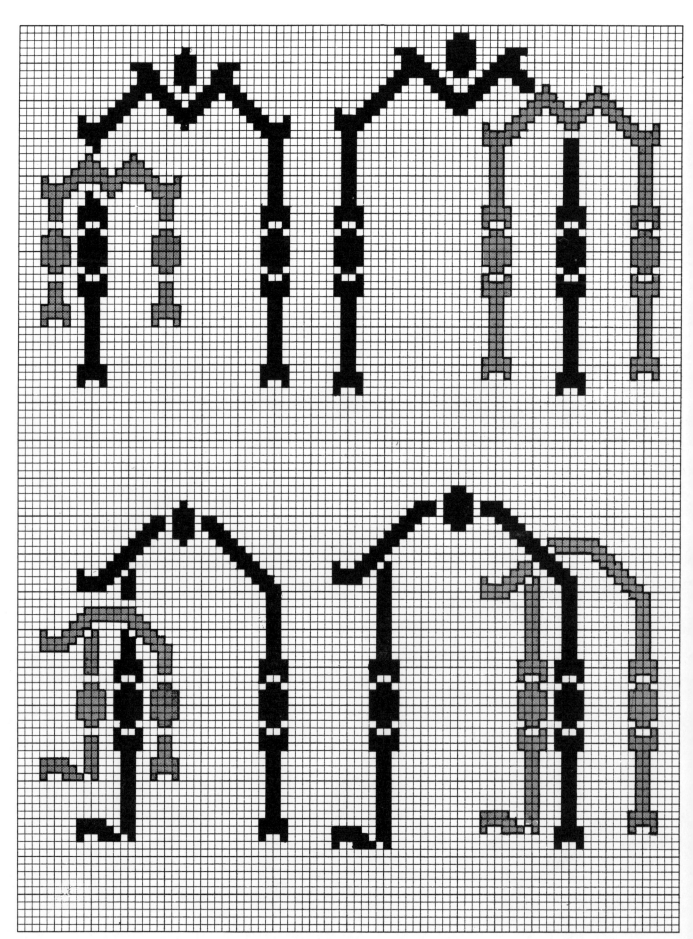

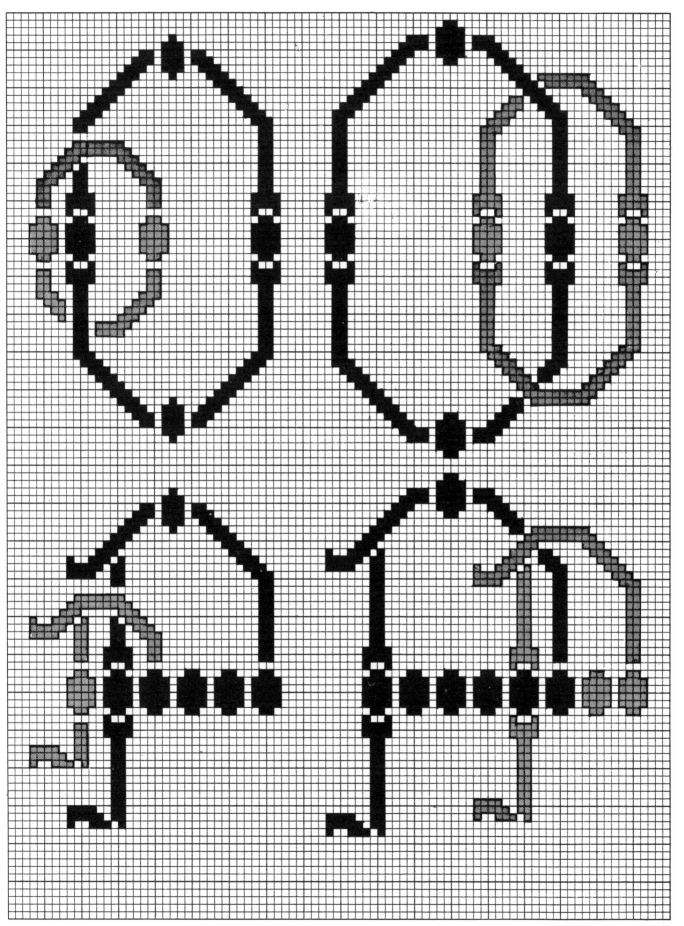

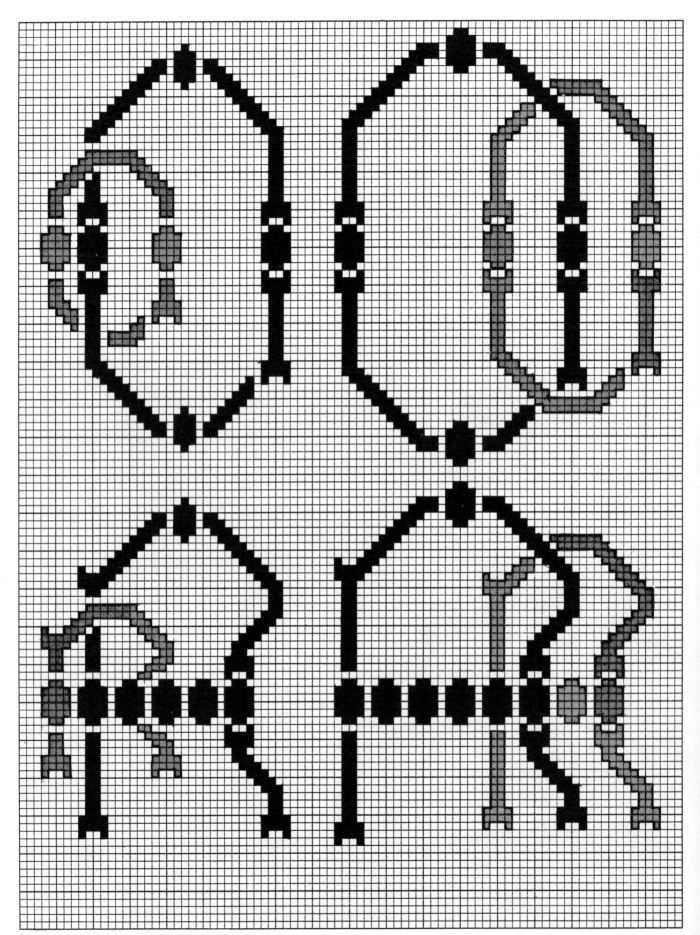

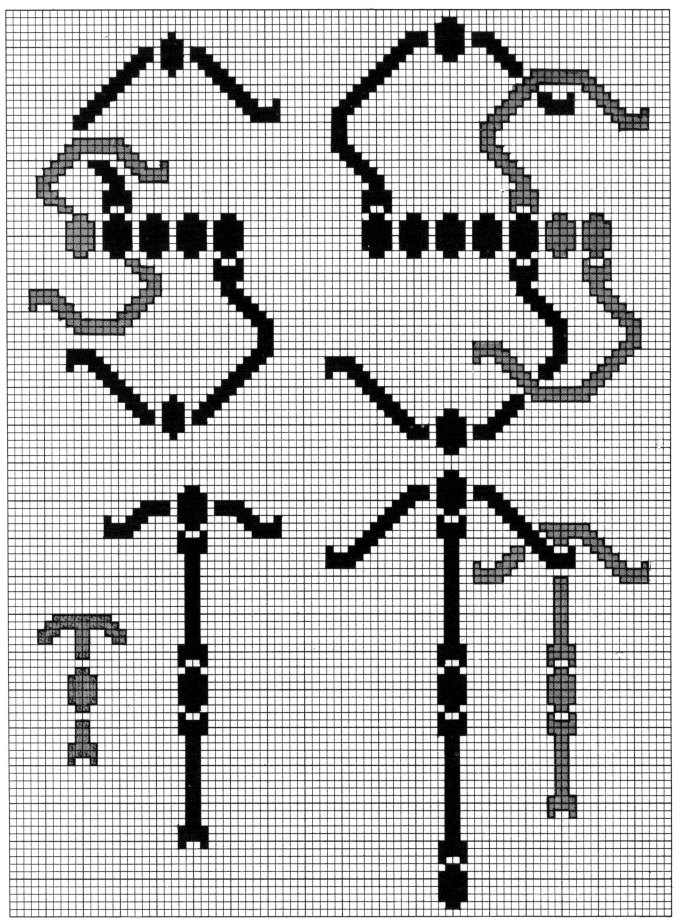

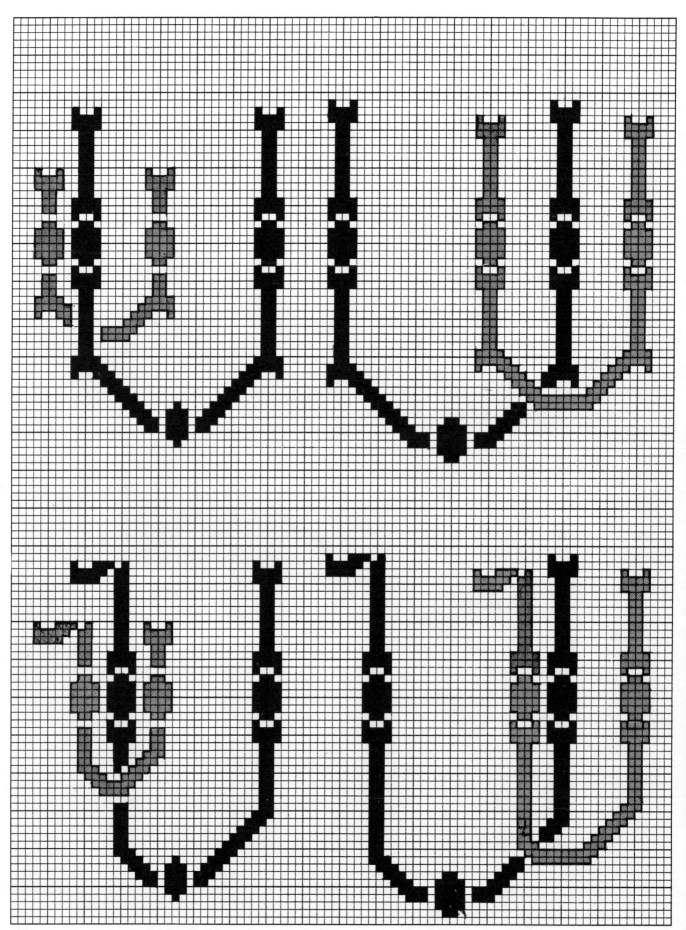

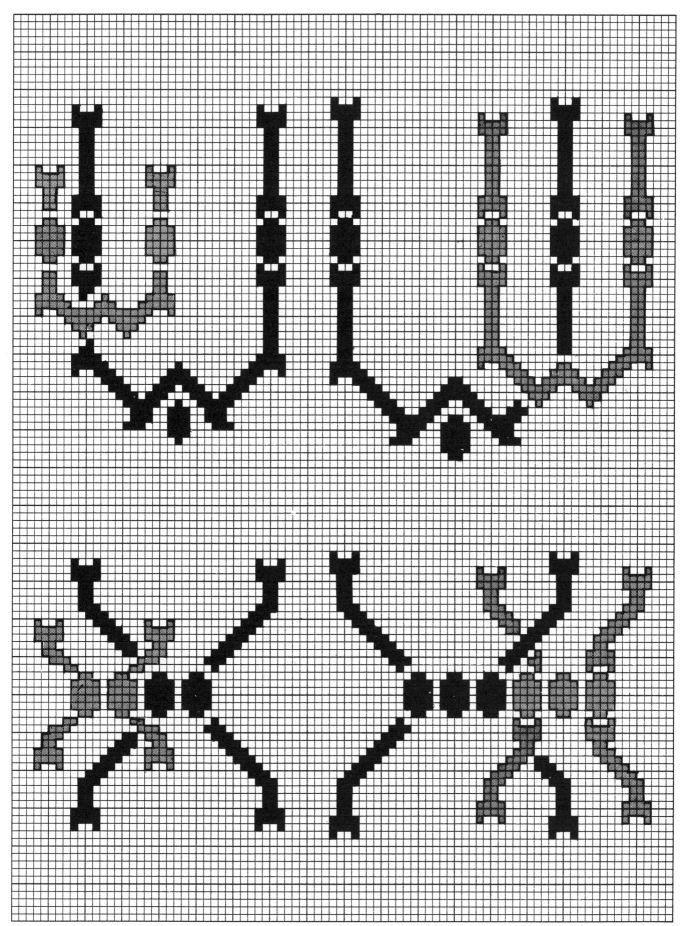

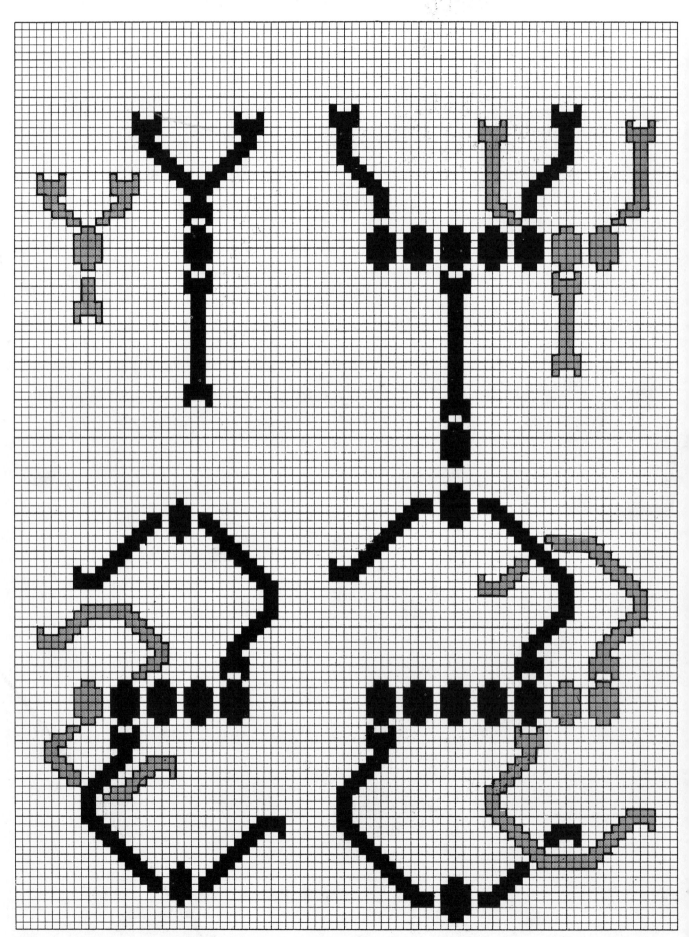